WHOLEHEARTED!

WHOLEHEARTED!

TENDING YOUR HEART
Through
BEING DISCIPLED BY JESUS

Rick and Diane Bewsher

XULON PRESS

Xulon Press
2301 Lucien Way #415
Maitland, FL 32751
407.339.4217
www.xulonpress.com

Printed in the United States of America.

ISBN-13: 978-1-5456-4219-1

Contents

Introduction

We are in an increasingly complex and challenging world. How critical it is then, for every follower of Jesus to know that the path to genuinely enjoying a life of intimacy with Him and thriving in the purpose He created us for is essentially very simple. Yes, it is stretching at times, but He is eager to help us every step of the way.

Who is this book written for?

- If you are hungering for more reality, depth and intimacy with Jesus.
- If you don't know that as a believer you can enjoy two-way conversation with God and find encouragement, healing and freedom in every area of your life, and so discover the true heart of our Father.
- If you have experienced severe trials and wounds and are wavering in your confidence in God, perhaps even struggling with anger and disappointment toward Him.
- If you have faithfully served and sought to follow God but know you need to experience a deeper place of rest, renewal and joy in your life with Him.
- If you know you have been running on empty.
- If you are losing your passion for Jesus and finding it hard to stand against the tide of compromise.

What do we mean by *"tending"* your heart?

According to Webster's dictionary, to *tend* is to "watch or guard", "to hold and take care of" and "to be attentive to" and so we have drawn the term "tending your heart" from that very sobering scripture, Proverbs 4:23.

> *"Watch over your heart with all diligence, for from it flow the springs of life"* (NASB).

> *"Above all else, guard your heart, for everything you do flows from it"* (NIV).

> *"Guard your heart above all else, for it determines the course of your life"* (NLT).

The heart is who we are–our inner core. Our deepest thoughts, feelings, desires, dreams and will. Our conscience and intuitions and insights. The avenue of trust and intimacy with God. Our spiritual life.

> *Our words, thoughts and actions spring from the heart (Matthew 15:18,19).*

> *God alone knows clearly who we truly are. We don't. (Proverbs 21:2).*

Because the course of our lives so critically pivot on the condition of our hearts, and because only God sees clearly the depths of its condition, then

> *It is our conviction that it is only as we learn to be discipled by Jesus are we able to tend our hearts effectively.*

As the Lord said to Samuel, the prophet: *"God sees not as man sees, for man looks at the outward appearance, but the Lord looks at the heart"* (1 Samuel 16:7).

> *Your heart will take you much farther than your gift ever will. Cultivate a heart after God. Your heart will take you to your destiny or your heart will sabotage your destiny. Guard your heart.*
> Christine Caine - The A21 Campaign

Why This Book Was Written

A few years ago, it became clear that the Lord Jesus was eager for my wife, Diane and I to write this book. Again and again, we recognized how motivated He was to use the material contained here to draw us all into a lifestyle of dynamically encountering Him.

Beyond the revolution in our own experience, after decades of seeking to walk with God, we have received hundreds of testimonies of believers from all levels of maturity who have seen hindrances removed and discovered freedom to plunge into the enjoyable intimacy that Jesus died to provide. And, of course, as we encounter Him we are changed and find the overflow of His Spirit splashing onto those around us.

The chapters in this book build in a sequence and culminate in the chapter *Tending Your Heart* which is a simple guide to cultivate an ongoing lifestyle of connecting with Jesus in a dynamic way.

We wondered whether all too often we have made abiding in Jesus, walking with Him as our best friend, far too complicated and elusive. Jesus makes it clear that it need not be so. If we are weary, hungry or thirsty, He simply invites, perhaps even challenges us: *"Come to Me!"* (Matthew 11:28;

John 6:35; 7:37). Maybe we have tried and not been able to receive the abundant life He offers. We trust that the Holy Spirit will take what He has given us in these pages and make a way perfectly tailored for you so that your hearts may rejoice in His grace like never before.

As Diane and I have gathered with people from all walks of life to facilitate conversations with the Father, we would come away, time after time, stunned at how wonderfully He is able to meet each of us, filling our hearts with encouragement and new life, no matter the challenges of our background. More often than not, the most broken people, if coming with honesty and openness, would enjoy the sweetest encounters with His heart, see Him like never before, and would never be the same.

Important Caveat

We include conversations with God in this book and what we believe to be His responses. From the outset, we want to make it clear that we are learners, growing in our capacity to hear God clearly, and so we don't ever want to presume that what we understand to be God speaking is always beyond dispute. However, rather than including, on every occasion, "It seemed to me that God said," or, "I sensed this is what He was saying," these potentially cumbersome qualifications have usually been omitted. The same caveat applies to others who have reported to us their own conver-sations with God.

How to Gain the Most From This Book

Beginning with Chapter 2, each chapter ends with an exercise. If you want to be changed, don't bypass these! In this book, we endeavor to go beyond simply relaying infor-mation. The book's purpose is to facilitate encountering God

Himself, for that is how we are changed, and these exercises will be doorways for you to meet with Him.

Acknowledgments

We are very grateful for all the ways in which the Holy Spirit is at work in the worldwide body of Christ. In recent days, it appears that more than ever that He is drawing us into the purpose for which we are created–intimacy with Jesus Himself. Of course, we have learned much from the ministry of others and have tried to acknowledge sources. To protect privacy when sharing personal stories, names have sometimes been changed.

Endorsements

There are very few times when a revelation impacts us for the rest of our lives. This is one of them! Rick and Diane Bewsher's revelation in Tending Your Heart and the practical guidance and leadership they've given us all on a lifestyle of hearing from and partnering with God, has not only changed my own life but thousands of others we have the privilege to serve around the world. I know it will change yours too if you take the time to read, listen and apply the truths in this book.

Jimmy Seibert
Senior Pastor, Antioch Community Church, Waco, Texas
President, Antioch Ministries International

Wholehearted! has the potential to become a classic because it represents a lifetime of learning in the deepest principles of following Jesus. Some books are for reading and then find their way to the bookshelf, but this book should be kept close at hand for helping people find freedom, identity, and peace in Christ. I have seen countless people helped by Rick and Diane and their ministry to the church. I enthusiastically recommend this book to you.

Jamey Miller
Lead Pastor, Antioch Fort Worth

The goal of most Christian books is to inspire and inform those who read them. However, books that set out to also systematically teach a practice (in this case, "Tending Your Heart") that if embraced and applied will radically and permanently transform your walk with God, are few and far between. This is one such book!

Rick and Diane have incarnated in their own lives the principles of Tending Your Heart and it radiates from their own lives. The book is the fruit of what they have discovered, and I for one am delighted that it is now available to the global church. As the Lord said to Ezekiel, "Eat this book!"

Ray Mayhew
Church planter, author, and leadership trainer
(primarily UK, Middle East)

Hidden inside the pages of this book are keys to unlocking deep intimacy with Jesus that we are created to hunger and thirst for. Rick and Diane have laid out practical tools to help us be discipled by Jesus and reproduce this in others.

Scott R.
Pastor of international field workers

Rick's got this way of making Jesus seem so accessible and available. He helped the people in our church grow in their confidence that when Jesus says, "My sheep hear My voice," that He's talking about them. How wonderful it is to hear Jesus speak personally to you! Rick's been blessed with a way of making this powerful spiritual reality come alive.

Kirk Freeman
Lead Pastor, Crossbridge Community Church,
San Antonio, Texas

Some ways God has used
Tending Your Heart

I was first introduced to Tending Your Heart 8 years ago when I was in a faith-based program for those recovering from substance abuse. I began going to the Father and asking Him what was wrong and why I had offense or why I was angry and it really helped me through that process of coming out of addiction and into freedom. But I didn't stop using it then. I still use it every day, years later. As a result, I have seen my relationship with the Father grow so much and so quickly. I am constantly talking with the Father, asking Him questions and getting His input and advice because who knows better than He does. He can see everything.

Samuel - missionary

My walk with Jesus is unlike anything I could have imagined due to the inner healing prayer I've had and through the exercise of 'tending my heart' continually over the past months. Jesus is more real, more personal, more loving and compassionate and gentle than I had ever experienced before. He has become to me the God He always was, but I had never known Him as. My walk with God has never been closer, and I've never trusted Him more.

Theo - Biblical lay counselor

I have freedoms that I never thought possible. An enormous weight has been lifted off my shoulders and shackles have been removed from my feet. Sins no longer tempt me that I had problems with for decades. I can now breathe deeply with joy in my heart, and I now know with confidence that Father loves me, Jesus is for me and will lead me every step of the way.

Pat - physician and worship leader

The vast majority of demonic attitudes and cravings that had daily hounded my soul and spirit disappeared overnight! And now I am left to wonder: What if I learned these truths as a young man? I am eternally grateful. Tending my heart has changed my life!

Charlie - church consultant and coach

I would cycle in and out of deep, deep depression every few days. [She had struggled with depression for years]. There hasn't even been a trace of depression in me - none! My life is totally different now, as I see myself as a daughter of God the Father. 'Tending Your Heart' has been the key to it all.

Christy - schoolteacher and Listening Prayer facilitator

CHAPTER 1

Searching for a Discipler

*B*eing discipled by Jesus? Seriously? What would that look like? Is that realistic or even scriptural? We invite you to join us on the ultimate adventure, not only of this lifetime, but beyond. This first chapter provides some personal background that sets the stage for the material we begin to introduce in Chapter 2.

I (Rick) was born in a small, remote mining town on the rugged west coast of Tasmania, Australia's island state. Down under down under, as I would say here in the USA. You could say it's the Wild West as it still boasts an Aussie rules football field of gravel–and no one wears padding! Tassie, as we call it, (pronounced "Tazzy"), is not on the way to any-where, unless you are planning on visiting the Antarctic. As I grew up on that island, I would easily identify with that Psalm (61:20): "From the ends of the earth I call to You when my heart is faint; Lead me to the rock that is higher than I."

Australia was first used by the English as a penal colony to alleviate London's overcrowded prisons, the first fleet arriving in 1788. Some of the worst criminals were sent to a tiny, isolated island in a huge harbor that had to be reached through the narrow opening called Hell's Gates, just down the coast from where I was born. Some escapees from there had even cannibalized each other to survive the 80 miles of dense vegetation and rough terrain to get to civilization. Our origins were not exactly the Pilgrims.

I am incredibly grateful that my parents loved Jesus, quite unusual in the Tasmanian culture. I was the middle of three boys, and it seemed obvious from an early age that my two brothers were destined to be engineers. While I had many interests, I was never sure what vocation I might pursue. I knew I wanted to help people and figured I may do some sort of Christian ministry. So, I graduated from the University of Tasmania with a degree in Clinical Psychology (counseling), only to find that this particular curriculum, in my opinion, never provided any real solutions to effectively deal with people's needs. It felt like we were offering Band-Aids for cancer.

After I graduated in 1971, I worked for a couple of years in the north of Australia. For a few months, I lived in a remote aboriginal community in *Crocodile Dundee* country where I had been asked to try and curb increasing vandalism among the youth. After that, I was a residential counselor in a boarding school in Darwin for children from the Outback where I was assigned to intervene because of tension between students and staff. For a year, I managed a brand new, 100-room YMCA hostel mainly occupied by transients, many with troubled pasts, although I had never managed anything in my life. At the same time, I was asked by the Darwin City Council to infiltrate and do a report on a large hippie community that was living illegally on a local beach for over a year. Continually confronted by people in difficulties that I was supposed to assist in some way, I knew I was in way over my head.

I had to deal with the suicide of a guy who I served notice on for not paying rent. I observed aboriginal friends succumb to the party scene of the whites. One night a guy staggered into my room, soaking wet from having swum ashore, to tell me he had just seen his friend drown in a boating accident. I had little confidence that I had much to offer, except to listen and do my best to empathize. Crippled by my own sense of inadequacy and the fear of man, sharing about Jesus was like pulling my own teeth.

I returned to Tasmania to visit my parents and intended to head to the USA and see what kind of practical pastoral training was available in a few seminaries that had been recommended. It was then that I was invited to join a Christian community near my hometown, Hobart, Tasmania's capital. At that time, Beth Shalom Community consisted of a pastor and his wife, who were popular counselors, and some singles. It offered full-time residential care for people wanting freedom from drugs and alcohol, those emerging from prison, some referred by local pastors and some from the psychiatric division of the Royal Hobart Hospital. I figured I would learn more practical skills here than in a classroom with a clipboard, so I stayed in Tassie and served in that community for five years.

With the Lord's grace, some people were helped and delivered, but frequently in me there would surface the cry—*there has to be more!* Why are we not more effective and seeing people radically transformed by the power of the resurrected Christ? Why is the church taking so little ground from the enemy? Why do we as His people so easily settle for flesh patterns, bondages and addictions that all too often seem to invalidate the good news? I had a lot of questions, but I felt no one understood my dissatisfaction or affirmed my hunger.

In 1977, I finally visited the USA. I was sent by Beth Shalom to check out other Christian communities, some of whom were doing similar work to us in rehabilitation. Based in Pasadena, California, I had 10 weeks. Secretly, I was hoping to find a discipler.

I had never had anyone disciple me. The church culture I had been raised in, never even presented such a notion as biblical, let alone modeled it. Yet, in my hunger to grow in God, I hoped I could find someone, some insightful prophet who could see into me, understand God's purpose for my life and speak to it, to give me hope and assurance. Although I had many acquaintances, in many ways I felt alone. Deep down, I longed for a mature brother with a rich experience of close friendship with Jesus, who would take me under his wing, walk with me, encourage and support me, correct me if necessary and share his wisdom; someone who would speak identity into me with authority so I could anticipate the future with confidence.

I remember visiting the church of a famous preacher in southern California, whose audio sermons on cassette tapes I had devoured, hoping he would notice me when I shook his hand at the door after the service. As it turned out, I never got close. I was awestruck and overwhelmed by the thousands there, and I felt like a naïve country hick to have such hopes.

I never did find that discipler, at least not in the way I was hoping for, but I did find my wife in Pasadena, California, hand-picked by Jesus, with the same heart as mine. But, that's another wild and wonderful story. We married later that year on Beth Shalom's sheep ranch overlooking a huge bay. Within 12 months, the Lord led us to leave our community and go to a church in London for a year as Bible students. At the end of that year, 1979, we returned to the USA and joined a sweet and vital fellowship with some of Diane's dear friends in central California where our daughter Bethany was born. We headed back to Tasmania in 1984 and spent most of the next 13 years longing to see the church there injected with new life. Most often, we had to find our encouragement as a family, and so we prayed for Jesus to build His church, His way and in His time. It was a very painful season, as we yearned for the healthy church community we had known in California. We also longed for Bethany to taste and see, to experience that for herself.

At long last, in 1997, Jesus told us to sell our home and real estate business, go to Los Angeles, buy a motorhome, start driving and He would show us where we were to live. And so, we did. Diane and I were eager to find close, meaningful, Jesus-centered fellowship. I had never been in a US motorhome, let alone driven one. I was intimidated to say the least, especially as I left the RV lot in our 34-foot rig and was engulfed with LA's rush hour traffic, driving on the right side of the road and towing our car. For the next 20 months, we traveled to 31 states and parked our motorhome with 80 hospitable, Christian families, the vast majority of whom we had never met before. What an incredible privilege!

With each encounter, we trusted that God would make clear to us the place He had prepared for us to settle. It may sound like a dream vacation, but it became emotionally taxing, not knowing whether each stop was it–the home He promised us. We determined to accept whomever He told us to be knit together with, as long as they loved Jesus. Keeping our hearts open, no matter what the situation looked like, also made us vulnerable. Time after time, He would prompt us to turn the ignition and keep moving. Aaargh!

As it happened, we did meet many who had been burned by the church, who had not only become gun-shy of any commitment to other brothers and sisters in Christ but had since found it more difficult to trust God Himself, sometimes blaming Him. Sadly, how often our view of God is molded and limited by our church experience, when He is so much kinder and more merciful than we can imagine!

For the most part, we met wonderful believers all over the US and yet He led us to stop in Virginia for over two years, miles from the nearest fellowship with which we had any links. We were confused. We were not Lone Rangers. Why had Jesus led us half way around the planet and kept us on our own? And we were a small family of three at that. We *longed* for fellowship. Diane remembers walking through Wal-Mart clinging to the shopping cart for support as she felt the pain of the absence of brothers and sisters in Christ with whom we could share life. I began to wonder whether it would have been better to stay in our home on the beach in Tassie. We didn't know of anyone else led this way, and we sure wouldn't recommend it. But, according to the light we had, we had followed where He led. I would protest to the Lord: *What about 1 Corinthians* (12:20, 21)? *We are members of one body. We need other members that we can be joined with.* The only response I sensed was: *Trust Me.*

The Wilderness

The wilderness has a way of sifting our hearts and purifying our motives; what it is that drives us. Was I proud, independent, exclusive, judgmental? Was I so hard-hearted that I couldn't hear Him? Did I have my fingers in my ears?

Despite the questioning, I knew God was up to something. I just hoped I would prove faithful. I had absolutely no idea just how helpful what He was doing in me would prove to be, for others, as well as myself.

In Colossians 1:18 it says that Jesus is head of the body, the church. Then, in 2:19 it says we are to *hold fast to the head.* Not the members, by the way! He kept reminding me of this phrase again and again. As we hold fast to Jesus, listen to and respond to Him, He will supply the church, hold it together and help it grow. It was true, that for years we had been forced to depend upon Jesus alone, without the encouragement and accountability of fellowship. We had to trust Him as our shepherd when nothing seemed to make sense, and our best efforts didn't seem to make much difference. Countless times I would grab the guitar, and we would sing as a family–*In Your time, in Your time, You make all things beautiful in Your time.* And the old favorite that never gets old, *Great is Your Faithfulness,* even if we sang it close to tears.

It's so much easier to trust Him if He makes it clear what He is teaching us, the purpose behind it and how long it will take. But then, that may not take much faith. We can just gut it out. But it's when we have no idea what He is up to, what His specific purpose is, and where He is leading, that we have the opportunity to simply trust in the kindness of His heart for us, even when it's painful. Graciously, He helped us cling to Him. We had nowhere else to turn, nor did we want to. I used to think, *well maybe He's refining me in this fire*, but all I could see was my flesh, like scum, coming to the surface. I had to learn to trust Him there as well, that He was capturing my heart despite the lack of fruit that I thought should have been more obvious.

So, what can we gain from our wilderness experiences? Think of the Israelites doing circles in the desert for 40 years. There are no footprints in the sand, often no role models to follow that have walked that particular way. There are no signposts. The wilderness is not a time to seek direction. They wandered in the wilderness. Jesus Himself was led about in the wilderness. Nor are there any mileage markers. This is not a time to assess our spiritual progress, to take our own pulse, to see if this journey is worth it. The scenery is often monotonous, so there's not so much distraction. Often those things that we may be tempted to look to for meaning and fulfillment, like

7

relationships, money, recognition or influence, prove illusory. Hopefully, we recognize the mirages for what they are.

So, what is the point of getting out of bed in the morning? The pillar of cloud moves, and where the cloud is there is covering, provision–and the tent of meeting (Exodus 40:34). "There I will meet with you … and I will speak to you" (25:22). In our deserts, God invites us to discover and experience the rivers of joy and vitality in knowing Him as our closest friend (Isaiah 43:20b, 21).

The wilderness is all about capturing our hearts, so we will learn to find our faithful Father and respond to Him. It's all about staying heart-connected with Him. It's an invitation to intimacy. And as we enjoy Him, we discover what we are made for, or rather, who we are made for. Only by His persistent grace, Diane and I can say that with all the ways He was leading that made little sense at the time, and with all the dry and painful times we seemed to stumble into, it never occurred to us to question the Father's love for us. We never expected that following Jesus would be easy.

Pursuing the Church or Jesus?

For many years, my focus and energy had been directed toward the pastoral needs of the church–wanting to see us all become healthier and more honoring to Jesus. Perhaps that was because, in my experience, all too often the church seemed to be one of the great stumbling blocks to people encountering Jesus–and obviously I was part of that one worldwide body. To both Diane and I, it seemed that time and again, Jesus would be misrepresented or squeezed out altogether.

A major shift in this church focus occurred when an elderly brother in Canada shared with me the story of Jacob.

After leaving home, having deceived his father and stolen his brother's blessing, Jacob had an encounter with God, but responds: "How awesome is this place," and called the place Bethel–the house of God (Genesis 28:17). He made a vow that if he was blessed, "then the Lord will be my God." 20 years later, after serving his unscrupulous uncle and perhaps recognizing his own reflection, he had another encounter with God at Peniel: "I have seen God face to face" (32:30). Jacob then returned to Bethel, but this time he called it *El Bethel* – the *God* of the house of God!

I recognized that God was doing the same with me, also after 20 years, diverting my goal away from wanting to see the church healed and transformed, and bringing me back to Jesus Himself, to be preoccupied with Him, whose church it was. As King David discovered: "My soul waits in silence for God only ... My soul thirsts for You" (Psalm 62:1; 63:1).

Furthermore, I was beginning to grasp that as we prioritize seeking to fix the church, we usually encounter our flesh, our own and others, and end up frustrated and disillusioned. But if pursuing Jesus is our primary desire, seeking above all else to know Him, very often we will also find others who are pursuing Him–His church. Beyond that, only as we attentively listen to the architect, builder, shepherd and head of the church, would we know how to partner with Him and accomplish what is on His heart.

Often, I would be discouraged at how far we, as God's people, fall short in representing Him faithfully. Time and again, it seemed to me, the church was shaped by a charismatic personality, our business acumen, our common sense, our preferences. But the resulting predictability I knew was a sign of artificiality and not the handiwork of the infinitely creative God whose signature of originality and spontaneity is true life.

It was during one of these discouraging times that the Lord spoke to me from Isaiah 42:4, which speaks of His Servant, Jesus. "He is never disheartened or crushed!" But how can that be possible? Jesus sees with absolute clarity the things we do as His church that displease Him. Wouldn't He be far more disheartened than us?

As I asked Jesus about it, He told me that He was never discouraged because He kept His eyes on what the Father was doing, and that work will always ultimately succeed and last. He said I was discouraged because I was preoccupied with what man was doing in the church. If I kept my eyes on Him, asked Him what He was doing and partnered with Him, then I would be kept from being disheartened. As Jesus said, He will build His church (Matthew 16:18). He will get His bride and she will be His delight (Revelation 19:7; Song of Songs 4:7, 9).

I was beginning to find that as I asked God to speak, and listened, that He gave me insight and keys that totally changed my perspective, giving me hope and ways to cooperate with Him that opened news doors of fulfillment, purpose and joy in the journey.

The End of the Search

At long last, in 2001, He led us from Virginia to a small fellowship in central Texas. I fell to my knees and cried like a baby when He told me. Nevertheless, it wasn't a honeymoon getting close and personal with other believers. Far from it. It turned out to be the most difficult and painful time of our lives to that point. There was sin in the camp. But the Holy Spirit had to do some surgery on us too–big time. It's surprising how much He is able to gain in messy situations if we are placing our hope in Him. Although Diane and I didn't know it at the time, He was laying foundations for healing and wholeness that we had never imagined.

Because of my desire to help people, I had always been eager to learn from any counseling ministry that produced ongoing transformation. A young couple from our fellowship, visited Waco, a 90-minute drive away, for some marriage counseling. When they returned, deeply impacted, I asked the guy what kind of advice they received. I had no idea that what he was about to tell me would begin a revolution in my heart that would inject a dynamic in my walk with Jesus, and that would eventually, through Diane and I, impact thousands.

In effect, here's what he said:

> *Actually, he didn't really counsel us.*
> *He just helped us hear from Jesus–and*
> *it was amazing!*

It was like the penny dropped. Or perhaps a better analogy: like a gentle shower that built into a torrential downpour. After all these years of trying to figure out what kind of counseling was the most helpful, I had essentially overlooked the fact that God Himself is called the "Wonderful Counselor" (Isaiah 9:6). Suddenly, it seemed so obvious. No wonder I was never fully satisfied with any counseling methodology I had tried or observed.

But before I became too carried away with the idea of motivating others to listen to Jesus for counsel, I realized I needed to get my own act together and listen to Him more intentionally myself. Of course! How could I offer anyone else an experience if I only knew the theory? Years earlier He had told me: *Rick, if you only know something in your head, you can't expect it to get below the necks of anyone else! You need to know the reality in your own heart and then I can reach the hearts of others.*

The Lord was using my motivation to help others to capture me in deeper ways for Himself. At the same time, in His kindness, Jesus had also been doing profound work in Diane, and we found He had brought us both onto the same page when it came to our desire to cultivate a lifestyle of listening to our Lord.

So, here began the most exhilarating adventure of our lives, and this book shares the heart of what we have learned, thus far, with Jesus as our Discipler. And we are ruined for anything less.

If you long to grow in your confidence in the heart of the Father and in your value to Him, then this is book is written for you. He promises to fill the hungry, and our desire and prayer is that this simple and practical volume will be used by Him to help you encounter His heart.

CHAPTER 2

Invitation to Intimacy

*L*iving on a pristine beach in Tasmania was a never to be forgotten pleasure. We knew we were being treated like the kids of a king. The sun and moon would rise shimmering over the bay where we would take our dinghy for a catch. I'll never forget one particular Good Friday netting 22 large salmon off the reef right in front of our home or snorkeling there for seafood with our daughter Bethany. We had a sense this was only for a season, but we had absolutely no idea where the Lord would lead us.

Never in our remotest dreams did we ever imagine God would take us to the middle of Texas, living down the end of a dirt road that wouldn't even show up on GPS. It was the state's worst school district and not exactly a choice area for a home, but this is where the Lord had clearly led us. So, we designed a house on a piece of graph paper and built it on a few cheap acres in the woods near some others in the fellowship. Our friends nearby called their road, crowded with mobile homes, *Stretch Lane*. Boy, was that the truth!

After six years, the Holy Spirit led us to move to Waco and to another fellowship where it began to dawn on us that finally, this long journey and the experiences He had taken us through, were all coming together. Until then, we had no idea how well the Lord was shepherding us. And what was He shepherding us into? Simply, intimacy with Him–in ways we had never anticipated. It was nothing short of revolutionary.

So, let's jump into how we can, very simply, cultivate a lifestyle of encountering God and the life-changing adventure of discovering Jesus as our Discipler.

As Jan Johnson says in *When the Soul Listens* (p.192): "Nothing can create a spiritual life for us–not the sermon, not dynamic worship, not a devotional guide, not the next book by a favorite author. God calls us to be discipled by Christ."

To thrive in this life and fulfill our destiny, there is nothing more critical than true friendship with God–intimacy with Him. It's actually why we were created. If we miss Him, we miss everything.

Perhaps our greatest fear is being left alone. Jesus, speaking of the Holy Spirit, said, "He ... will be in you. I will not leave you as orphans; I will come to you," (John 14:17, 18). And then, His last words to His disciples were, "I am with you always" (Matthew 28:20). Clearly, He has made the way for us to be fulfilled in our friendship with Him.

Still, even as believers, we can go through the outward motions, the accepted religious norms, and never really get to know Him or allow Him to get very close to us. These days more than ever, we hear songs about intimacy with Jesus– "the riches of Your love will always be enough ... nothing compares to Your embrace." Potent lyrics. Is this truly our experience?

What do we mean by intimacy with God? This is how I experience it. First, it's where we are totally free to share our hearts with Jesus; to be gut level honest with Him about our feelings, our doubts, fears and struggles, as well as pour out our worship, gratitude and love on Him. Second, where our relationship with Him is often severely lacking is where we are able to really *receive His heart for us.* Intimacy is all about a heart-to-heart connection with the living God. As we grow in this intimacy, there may, at times, be less need for words as we simply connect with and enjoy one another in the silence.

Because this intimacy is what we were created for, it's what the Father wants more than anything else. How about us? The question isn't so much: Did we have "time with Jesus" today?

The question is: Did we enjoy Him?

> *Do we spend time with Him because we feel we should or because we want to?*

Furthermore, do we have time with Him to improve ourselves, to feel more spiritual or because we want to meet with Him?

Beyond that—do we want to connect with Him *during* the day? Is this our lifestyle? Or is a "time with Jesus" something where we check in with Him then go off and do our day? And then, as we climb into bed, think back and say, *Well I hope that was a good day.* Or, are we learning to stay connected with Him and partner with Him throughout our day?

In the last 40 years, Diane and I have had our share of trials and struggles, periods of isolation and aloneness when there was limited access to healthy fellowship and encouragement. If we were depending on what was going on around us in the body of Christ, or placing our hope in our circumstances, we would not be in a good place, either with God or each other.

But through it all, and probably because we spent years without the rich, life-on-life fellowship we longed for, by His grace we learned to connect with the Father. Most that was life-giving for us was the result of what we received from God, occasionally through others, but most often directly from Him. His encouragement is what has sustained us, excited us and motivated us to get to know Him more. Still, even after all these years, we both feel like a couple of kids barely beginning to jump into this amazing adventure of sharing our hearts and our lives with our Father.

So, practically speaking, what does intimacy with Father God look like? Do you feel like you have to perform to please Him? What the Father invites us into, is the difference between being a housemaid and a beloved wife. It's the difference between being a servant or even a soldier and being a beloved son. It's where our relationship with Him means more to us than what we do. We simply enjoy being with each other, sharing hearts in conversation.

The Father wants heart conversation with us far more than we can imagine!

Jesus, in Matthew 4:4, says: "Man shall not live on bread alone, but on every word that proceeds out of the mouth of God." He is quoting from Deuteronomy 8 where God is sharing with His people through Moses (vs. 2, 3) that the reason He had them in the wilderness for 40 years was to humble them, for them to learn what was in their hearts, and then to make them understand that man is to live by everything proceeding from His mouth. In essence, God was saying to His people: I had you in the desert 40 years, so you would learn to live listening.

Our Father created us to live by what we hear from Him— listening to and responding to Him. Now this is far more than listening to Him for instruction, guidance and direction. This is being attentive to Him for encouragement, comfort, affirmation and identity that perhaps we have never been told but have longed to hear. But even more than this, the Father wants us to get to know and take delight in Him!

Most of my life I have enjoyed worshiping God, thanking Him for His kindness and faithfulness, and I would pray about different needs. Some years ago, I was returning from a walk in the woods near our home having had one of these focused times with Jesus and felt like He said to me:

Rick, I really enjoy you sharing with Me and I like to hear what's on your heart, but when you are finished talking, it's like you hang up on Me!

> *I have so much I want to share with you,*
> *but you keep cutting Me off!*

Those few words began a most dramatic change in my walk with Jesus: learning to be inwardly still, to tune in and listen to hear what is on His heart. He loves to hear our hearts, but it's when I hear His heart–that's what changes my life! That's what rocks me. That's what sticks with me. That's what motivates me. That's what sets me free. And that's what stirs my desire to know Him better and listen to Him more.

How can we have a deep friendship with someone if we are doing all the talking?

In all of this, Jesus Himself is our role model.

In John 5:19, He says He didn't do anything without watching the Father. In John 8:26, 28, Jesus says He didn't say anything on His own initiative but only spoke what He heard from the Father. Jesus lived His life watching the Father with the eyes of His heart, with sanctified imagination, and listening to what He had to say. Everything we see in the life of Jesus on this earth was the result of His continual depen-dence upon and response to His Father's initiative.

And this is how we were created to live. "The one who says he abides in Him [Christ] ought himself to walk in the same manner as He walked" (1 John 2:6).

In Luke 10:38-42, we read where Jesus is talking to Martha who is busy serving, but who is anxious and uptight. It's easy for us to identify with Martha. At least she is trying to help and do something useful. But Martha is also frus-trated with her sister Mary whom she feels should stop sitting around and help her. In fact, she starts bossing Jesus around and telling Him to pull Mary into line.

But Jesus told Martha that Mary was doing the one thing necessary! Now when Jesus said there is really only one thing necessary, we should let it sink in so that His words don't just bounce off but make sure we really are getting what He is saying.

All we are told about Mary in this incident is that she was seated at Jesus' feet, listening. She was not walking through the room, preoccupied as she was listening. She was seated. It was a settled issue for Mary that nothing was more important than giving Jesus her full attention and lis-tening to what He had to say to her. She was focused on Jesus and listening to Him. It sounds similar to how Jesus lived before the Father, doesn't it?

We see this same heart in King David, the greatest warrior king of Israel, the "man after God's own heart" as he shares with us His deepest motivation. "One thing I have asked of the Lord, that I will seek: That I may dwell in the house of the Lord forever, to behold the beauty of the Lord and to meditate (lit. inquire) in His temple" (Psalm 27:4). More than anything, David wanted to fix his heart on the beauty of the Lord, ask Him questions and listen.

> *In our relationship with Jesus, there is simply nothing more critical or life-giving than listening to Him, hearing what is on His heart and responding to Him.*

Before we go on, it needs to be said that to live listening doesn't mean that God wants us to live like robots, immobilized unless we can say, *God told me.* A listening heart is an attentive and responsive heart, no matter how the Lord chooses to interact with us. Maybe as I'm pulling weeds I recognize the Lord's kindness is drawing my attention to things which are choking my life with Him and I need to take some action. I may see a neighbor and feel a burden or receive an impression that I need to stop what I'm doing and go visit. While there will be many times when the Holy Spirit within will prompt us to stop and ask Him questions or just listen to Him, the fact remains that as we learn to stay yielded and attentive to the Spirit, He will faithfully reveal Himself and lead us, and we will find ourselves responding to Him, often living supernatural lives quite unconsciously.

The Pursuer

Here is something that I believe will help us more than anything else in growing in enjoyable intimacy with the Father. God is the initiator. He is the pursuer.

> *He is far more motivated to connect with us than we are with Him!*

If we feel like we have to get His attention, to twist His arm to get Him motivated to help us, and that He is not really that

19

interested in getting close to us, then we will be easily dis-couraged and find it hard to continue to press in to know Him, especially if we feel like we are not making much progress. But, if we come to recognize that we are not waiting for Him, He is waiting for us to respond to His relentless initiatives, then it can change everything. In one sense, the thought that we are waiting for Him is crazy! He is the initiator and always has been! When we were dead in sin, walking in rebellion, He died for us (Ephesians 2:1-9).

Why did Jesus die? Ultimately, what was His purpose in dying for us? Matthew 27:50, 51 tells us that after Jesus com-mitted His spirit to the Father while on the cross, the very first thing that happened was that the veil, the entrance into the Holy of Holies, was *ripped* from top to bottom. What we see here is a crystal-clear demonstration of the strength of His passion! The veil was ripped from top to bottom, showing to all that God was doing this. It's like the Father was saying: *Finally! Enough of this system!* So, what is the point of all this? The ultimate focus of the temple was the Holy of Holies, and in Exodus 25:22 we are told: "*there I will meet with you… and I will speak to you…*" More than anything, the Father wants intimacy with us.

Previously, according to the laws given by God, only the High Priest could enter the Holy of Holies once a year (Hebrews 9:7). But Jesus gave up His life so that, cleansed by His blood, we can all enter the Holy of Holies with confi-dence and expectancy (Hebrews10:19-22) and get as close to the Father as we want. What Moses enjoyed in Exodus 33:11 of "face-to-face" encounters with the living God, is now, through the massive price Jesus paid, made available to all who believe. This is not just for the 'spiritual' ones. He died once, for all! He died to bring us all to His Father (1 Peter 3:18).

We are now without excuse. Sin, weakness and shame have been overcome by pure grace. Jesus said: "It is finished!" Now it's our move! So, what's stopping us from taking Jesus at His word, taking Him up on His invitation and responding?

What Do We Believe When We Fail?

When we have blown it, rejected God's initiatives and turned our back on Him, do we still have the confidence to turn around, come to Him and know that His heart is still open to us? Jesus knew that self-condemnation would cause us to pull back in shame and He addresses this in what is probably the most loved story in Scripture because it strikes a chord in us all; the story of the prodigal son, in Luke 15. Really, it's the story of the prodigal's dad.

As James Bryan Smith says in *The Good and Beautiful God* (p.99): "The parable of the prodigal son should really be called the parable of the father's love. The word *prodigal* means "recklessly extravagant." We attach the word to the younger son, the one in the story who spends all of his inheritance on sinful living. But it is the father who is recklessly extravagant, offering his wealth to an ungrateful son and lavishly loving the son when he returns."

Though the younger son wanted his inheritance more than a relationship with his dad, couldn't wait for his father to die, virtually spat in his face and took his money before it was rightfully his,

> *Jesus reveals the heart of His own Father.*

It's almost like He is saying: *Look at this! You have never seen a father like Mine! You have never experienced love like this!* What do we notice? The father never closed his heart

21

to his son. We could understand a dad being grieved and heartbroken with his son's selfish choices and being blind to his father's love, but nevertheless, eventually accepting the reality and resigning himself to getting on with his life, saying: *At least I have one son left.*

Instead, we read: "But while he was still a long way off, his father saw him." Clearly, this father was not just moving on with his life. Instead, he must have been persistently watching and longing for his son's return. Life was not the same without him. Once he saw him in the distance, he had compassion and ran to him. I have heard that it was not dignified in that culture for an older man, the head of a household, to run, probably having to pull up his robe and expose his legs. In that moment, he cared only for his son. He embraced him "fell on his neck" (KJV), "threw his arms around him" (NIV) and kissed him. What sweet relief and joy for the father to hold him again and know that his son had returned to him by choice to receive his love. He couldn't contain his exuberance. He had to throw a party.

It is salutary for us to consider the implications for us, as sons of the Father. No matter what the prodigal did, the father always called him *my son!* Even though the older son refused to call him his brother, the father made it clear that no matter what the younger son had done, nothing would change the fact that he was his son. He was committed to him as his father and his heart was always for him. If his son wanted to return home repentant, he would always be welcome.

We could easily imagine the dad waiting at the gate as his son approached, ready to dress him down harshly: *You have made life difficult for all of us. You can't expect me to trust you now, so you will be on probation. Work starts at five am. You can use the bunkhouse with the other servants and time will tell whether you really are repentant. If your attitude is genuine and you prove yourself, then we will see if you are worthy to come back into my house.*

No condemnation or shame is laid on the repentant son, nor is he required to perform for approval. Neither is that the heart of our heavenly Father towards us. Jesus' punishment on our behalf paves the way for us to come with repentant hearts, yes, but without fear of rejection, fully confident of a warm welcome right back where we belong in our Father's embrace. We can imagine the prodigal on his way back home dragging his feet with his head down, ashamed. If he really knew what was in the heart of his dad, he also would have been running, with tears in his eyes, yes, but with arms open to receive his full acceptance.

Why the Distance Between Us and God?

Maybe you have seen an old painting of Jesus standing at a door knocking. It's based on Revelation 3:20. No, it's not some criminal inside. It's the church. He is asking them to let Him come in so that they can enjoy a meal together. In effect, what He is saying is, *I want to share My heart with you and I want you to share your heart with Me.* Jesus is the one who wants to get in. We are the ones who have closed the door in His face.

> *He wants us to want Him.*

He will never violate us. He could kick the door down or vaporize it for that matter. But He's just gently knocking. The divine restraint is staggering! He so values us and honors us. He will rarely push His way into our hearts. He longs for us to respond, open up to Him and welcome Him in so He can come closer with no barriers between us.

The Initiator

Take a look at this incredible passage that describes our salvation.

> God said: ". . . on the day you were born your navel cord was not cut, nor were you washed with water for cleansing, you were not rubbed with salt or even wrapped in cloths. No eye looked with pity on you, to do any of these things for you, to have compassion on you. Rather, you were thrown in an open field... *I saw you squirming in your blood... I said 'Live!'* ...yes, I said to you while you were in your blood, *'Live!'* You were naked and bare. *I covered your nakedness. I swore to you and entered into a covenant with you,* so you became Mine... *I bathed you* with water, washed off your blood from you and *anointed you* with oil. *I clothed you... I adorned you* with silver... you were exceedingly beautiful and advanced to royalty... your beauty was *perfect because of My splendor which I bestowed on you,* declared the Lord God."
>
> (Ezekiel 16: 4-14; emphasis added)

Who doesn't want to know a God like this? Who doesn't want to know a father like this? Whether we are in touch with this or not, the fact is we were all in a ditch, squirming in our blood, helpless and filthy—and He did it *all!* Even our desire to respond to Him, He put it there.

In my mid-twenties, for several years I managed a sheep ranch in Tasmania and I learned that sheep are pretty helpless and defenseless. They are utterly dependent on the kindness of the shepherd. David, the psalmist lived with them and identified with them. Psalm 23 is perhaps the best known, but I wonder how much we appreciate the heart of our shepherd?

The Lord is *my shepherd*
I shall not want
He makes me lie down in green pastures
He leads me beside quiet waters
He restores my soul
He guides me in paths of righteousness for His name's sake
Even though I walk through the valley of the shadow of death
I fear no evil for *You are with me*
Your rod and Your staff they comfort me
You prepare a table before me in the presence of my enemies
You have anointed my head with oil
My cup overflows
Surely goodness and loving kindness will *follow me* all the days of my life
And I will dwell in the house of the Lord forever.

(Psalm 23; emphasis added)

Jesus calls us His sheep. Exactly what is the sheep doing in this psalm? All the sheep is doing is watching the shepherd, seeing where he is going, responding to him and following his lead. The shepherd takes all the initiative. Jesus says *you will have no lack if you look to Me and follow Me.* Are we prepared to live like dependent sheep? Do we trust Him to meet our deepest needs—in His way and in His time? He'll even help us respond to His leading. Do we trust Him to do even that?

We really can live this way. And if we learn to trust Him like this it will eliminate our fear and striving. We will be delivered from the performance trap. We don't need to strive to perform for approval when we know we have a shepherd like this. His perfect love, when we take it to heart, overcomes all fear of not measuring up or missing out.

To see His heart for us truly changes everything. So, we can have confidence in coming to Him with no fear of rejection, listening to Him with expectancy, fully assured that He will meet the needs of our heart.

The Goal of the Journaling Exercises

At the end of each chapter is an exercise. If you want to be changed, don't bypass these. This book is not about relaying information. Its purpose is to facilitate encountering God Himself, for that is how we are changed, and these exercises will be doorways for you to meet with Him.

While we offer these exercises, when we think of friendship with God, we certainly don't want to present a methodology and reduce our relationship with Him to some trite formulas. These are simply some handrails to help us move forward in places where we may have felt hindered. Our goal is to go far beyond providing tools to solve our issues, but to enjoy connecting with and partnering with God Himself.

BRINGING IT HOME

Below is a selection of scriptures that focus on God's desire for dialogue with us. Perhaps one or more will capture your attention. You may want to delve deeper by considering:
What is this verse saying about God's desire for me?
How can I respond to God's initiative to experience His purpose for me?
How could this impact my life?

Matt.27:51 Access to Holy of Holies.

Ex.25:21,22 I will meet with you ... speak to you.

Matt.4:4 We fully live by what He speaks. Is.55:3 listen that you may live.

Jn.8:26,28 Jesus, our role model.

Lu.10:39,42 The one thing necessary.

Ps.27:4 One thing I do ... behold ... and
   [lit.] inquire (asking questions and listening)

Ps. 95:7,8 Today if you want to hear His voice, do not harden your hearts.

Jer.33:3 Call to Me, I will answer you, I will tell you great ... things which you do not know.

Is.58:9,11 You will cry, and He will say, "Here I am" ...The Lord will guide you continually.

Is.30:21 You will hear a word from your Teacher ... whenever you turn.

Is.1:18 Come now and let us reason together.

Jn.10:27 My sheep hear Me. Jn.8:47.

Jn.10:3 He calls His own sheep by name.

Is.9:6 Counselor, Jn.20:17, your Father,

Jn.15:14 My friends. (Includes conversation.)

Prov.8:32 Happy are those who listen and respond.

Ps.81:13 The enemy is quickly subdued.

Check RESOURCES (p.241) *Hearing God and Expectancy* for more scriptures on hearing God.

ASK HIM AND JOURNAL

Father, what have I believed about intimacy with You?

How do You want to encourage me to grow in enjoying intimacy with You?

What do You want me to do to cooperate with You and experience more intimacy with You?

If you had difficulty doing this exercise and hearing the Father's encouragement to you, then read on!

CHAPTER 3

The War Over Intimacy

*T*he enemy knows that intimacy with us is the one thing above all else that God wants, that heart-to-heart connection with us is His chief desire. The enemy also understands that if he can kill our intimacy with God, we will not be any threat to his kingdom whatsoever. As Jesus said: "He who abides in Me and I in him, he bears much fruit; for apart from Me you can do nothing" (John 15:5).

Busy "for God"?

One of the ways the enemy tries to kill intimacy is by keeping us busy doing things which we may justify are "for God." But so often we are driven, seeking approval from God or trying to impress others because we have the need to be needed or recognized, or we are trying to feel good about ourselves, to feel validated. But God is not a harsh taskmaster. Perhaps we think we understand that He is not, but that's usually not the way we live.

> *God is not so focused on what we do,*
> *as what it is that motivates us.*

In Matthew 7:22, 23 Jesus says: "Many will say to Me on that day, 'Lord, Lord, did we not prophesy in Your name, and in Your name cast out demons, and in Your name perform many miracles?' And then I will declare to them, 'I never knew you; depart from Me you who practice lawlessness.'"

This is a heavy thought. In effect, what is Jesus saying? *I want your friendship. I want a relationship with you more than anything else. Service without Me means nothing to Me. In fact, you may even be opposing Me.*

In our enthusiasm and zeal, it is all too easy for us to charge off with our own ideas of how we think we can serve God, without tuning in and hearing what He has to say about how He wants us to respond.

Perhaps we can easily identify with Peter. He received revelation of Jesus from the Father Himself: "You are the Christ, the Son of the living God." Jesus then responded with that huge statement: "I will build my church" (Matthew 16:16-18). However, look at what happened merely six days later. "He was transfigured before them; and His face shone like the sun, and His garments became as white as light. And behold, Moses and Elijah appeared to them, talking with Him. And Peter answered [although he was not being addressed] and said to Jesus, 'Lord, it is good for us to be here; if You wish, *I will make* three tabernacles here, one for You, and one for Moses, and one for Elijah.' While he was still speaking, behold, a bright cloud overshadowed them; and behold, a voice out of the cloud, saying, 'This is My beloved Son, with who I am well-pleased; listen to Him!'" (Matthew 17:2-5; emphasis added).

Why does Jesus put us in challenging situations of need? So that we will turn to Him and find Him. To Jesus, it's all about relationship. Life is difficult. It's a divine set-up so that we will discover just how compassionate and capable He is to help us in those trials, so that we will be drawn to Him.

Primarily, it's not about fulfilling our call or our ministry. It's about knowing Him.

Jesus wants us to stay connected with Him, learning to partner with Him in our work. We can easily get in the habit of getting our work order from Him and heading off on our own to do it. Then we return and ask: *Is there anything else You want me to do?* Living this way, we shut Him out of most of our day! He wants us to invite Him into our work so He can join us there.

That's why in John 15:5 Jesus said that apart from Him, we can do nothing. Jesus said He could not do anything without His Father. Who are we to think we don't need to be as dependent as Jesus? Well actually, He and only He could have been independent, but His union with the Father was everything to Him. He had no desire to do anything without Him. Everything He did flowed from His relationship with the Father, responding to His initiative. Again, Jesus is the perfect role model for us.

When Jesus said "Abide in Me" that means *remain* in Me. Stay with Me 24/7. Don't just pay visits! If we stay connected with Him, He promises there will be much fruit – and it will last.

In Mark 3:13-15 the heart of Jesus is further revealed as we see His primary desire for His disciples before sending them out—which, of course, includes us.

> "And He went up to the mountain and summoned those whom He Himself wanted, and they came to Him. And He appointed twelve, *that they might be with Him,* and that He might send them out to preach, and to have authority…" (emphasis added).

Authority to share Jesus must first come from being with Him and learning how to partner with Him.

31

Here's another way we miss Him.

> *We can become so focused on serving God that we seek power to serve Him rather than seeking God Himself.*

We overlook the Giver in our preoccupation with building our 'spiritual' resume.

In 1979, Diane and I were in Switzerland camped by a stream at the foot of the magnificent Mount Eiger in a picture-perfect setting. I remember it well. But what remains far more vivid to this day was something Jesus spoke to me that pierced my heart and became a dramatic watershed in the trajectory of my life. As I have since experienced many times, it was simple, but it riveted me: *Rick, do you love Me?* His emphasis was on the word *Me.*

It began to dawn on me that what I really loved, what I really was excited about and motivated by was not really Jesus at all. I wasn't excited about Him as a person. What motivated me was what I thought I could do for Him, the part I hoped I could play in His kingdom, the role I might have in His purposes. It was all about me. Come to think of it as I'm writing this, it sounds just like the disciples comparing themselves to one another, even at the last supper, totally oblivious of Jesus and the cross He was about to face.

I was acting like an addict. You see I had opportunities to speak and share a little, and when people responded well, I was high as a kite. But, when people didn't show up or responded negatively, I was bummed. I was on a rollercoaster, driven by my own sense of inadequacy and the fear of man. I felt like He told me: *Rick, you have to get off this thing!*

and we are trying to prove something, or we are looking for a cool testimony to tell our friends, they will feel genuinely loved because we are responding to the unconditional love of God that we have received. We are not out for anything for ourselves. It's all for Him.

While in college, a friend of mine, Blake led a group of students on an outreach to Mongolia. He was eager to share the love of Jesus and the gospel on the streets and was excited about the possibility of seeing a church planted in the seven weeks of their summer break. On the third day he was playing basketball and dislocated his knee, so he was forced to spend virtually the rest of his time confined to the sofa in his room. Blake had learned to dialogue with the Father and process his heart with Him. He told Him of his frustration and said: *Surely my destiny is to change the world.* And the Lord responded: *Experiencing My embrace is your destiny!* So, he determined to receive this and trust and rest in Him.

He started worshipping and enjoying Jesus in his room and sensed the sweetness of His presence. After some time, two young Mongolian men came to visit, and they too were captured by the presence of Jesus. When Blake returned home, he told me that even though the Lord accomplished much on the streets in bringing people into the kingdom and raising up a young church, those two young guys who tasted the presence of Jesus with him became two of the stronger men in that move of God.

As we experience the beauty of Christ and the stunning depths of His kindness and power, it will put a consuming desire in us, a taste of Him that no efforts for Him or even righteous accomplishments will satisfy. Then, nothing else matters as much as staying connected with Him and responding to Him, whatever that looks like. Others will then sense Christ, not us, and be drawn to Him.

Hearing God

In James 1:5 it says that if you ask God for wisdom, He will give it to you–generously. It then goes on to say that you must ask without any doubt otherwise you can expect nothing! At first, I was discouraged. When am I going to have no doubt and perfect faith?

But the Father spoke to me and said something like this: *No Rick, you don't understand. Of course, I want to share My wisdom with anyone who asks. It's like I have a baseball and I want to throw it to you as soon as you ask, but when you ask Me, it's like your arms are crossed. You have no expectancy that I will give you wisdom right then.* It was true. I assumed I would read a book next month or bump into someone who would give me some good advice and so on, and of course He often does choose those avenues.

He continued: *If You really expect Me to deliver wisdom when you ask, you will have your catcher's mitt ready. Your mitt is expectancy. If I throw the ball and 'your arms are folded', your heart will never be in a position to receive what I want to give you.*

Since then, my experience has been that when I come to the Father expecting Him to meet my heart, He does. Of course, it may be in ways different than I expect. It may not always be in words. Sometimes He may show me that I need to be still and trust Him. He may indicate an action I need to take. I have learned that He knows what I really need, and I don't. But He always has something for me when I am open to immediately receive. When I am expectant, the ball is often in my mitt before I know it!

King David had an expectant heart. "In the morning, O Lord, You will hear my voice; In the morning I will prepare [a prayer and a sacrifice] for You and watch and wait [for You to

CHAPTER 4

The Nature of God's Voice

"This is My beloved Son,
with whom I am well pleased; listen to Him!"
(Matthew 17:5).

*H*ow do we grow in our friendship with God that we have been created for? Here is an excerpt from my (Diane's) listening journal when I asked the Father to give me His view of intimacy.

Intimacy can only exist when there is the intentional commitment on both sides to explore the relationship, not simply being together in one another's presence but choosing to open oneself to the searching gaze and mind of the other. I made you for intimacy. I long to know you (for you to open yourself and share yourself with Me) and be known by you.

Webster's Dictionary describes intimacy as close familiarity or fellowship, nearness in friendship, a familiar friend, one to whom the thoughts of another are entrusted without reserve, to love entirely without reserve or guardedness.

There is a huge difference between knowing about the Lord, knowing something of what my relationship with God is supposed to look like, and knowing God in an experiential and intimate way. It can be compared to reading a book and understanding only rationally some of the author's message, whereas it is much more meaningful to spend time with the author himself, to talk with him about his ideas and thoughts in a deeply personal and profound way.

To walk in an intimate friendship with God requires, at least partly, two-way conversation. Nonetheless, it needs to be said, that as we trust Him, we can also share hearts without using words, just as we can in human relationships.

Personally, I must intentionally listen to what God wants to say to me and give Him room to share all that He has on His heart. I am not just telling Him what I feel or need. I want my heart to receive what He says, embrace it, and then respond and live it out.

We are listening to voices all the time, whether we are aware of them or not. We listen to the voice of the world, the voice of the enemy and our un-renewed thoughts. They are like radio waves that are constantly broadcasting, competing for airtime to hinder us from hearing from the One whose words bring life. If we practice intentionally listening to the voice of God we will soon recognize any voice that is not His.

That brings us to the big question, especially with a new believer: *How do I learn to confidently know I am hearing the voice of God? What is His voice like?* Here are some simple guidelines, what we call the Litmus Test.

1. They will draw us to Jesus, to see more of His heart, causing us to want to follow and love Him more.
2. His words will never violate but easily align with Scripture. So, the more we know the Bible, the more the Holy Spirit can bring pertinent verses to mind to guide us. The more familiar we are with the heart of God and His ways revealed in Scripture, the more easily we will recognize Him when He speaks.

3. They will reflect the character of the Spirit: loving, joyful, peaceful, patient, kind, good and gentle (Galatians 5:22).
4. They will affirm the roles of the Holy Spirit: Helper, Encourager, Comforter, Teacher, Guide, Life-giver, Strengthener, Empowerer, Liberator, Revealer of Truth, Gift-giver.
5. The nature of God's thoughts will be spontaneous and ultimately positive, usually in the first person, such as, *I want you to know that I love you My child.*
6. He will never create confusion (1 Corinthians 14:33).
7. He will never bring condemnation or shame on His children (Romans 8:1). While at times there maybe a gentle rebuke or correction that will bring conviction, it's the kind of rebuke that produces a longing to come back to Him.

Here's an example from my journal of a gentle rebuke:

> *Lord at times I become drawn by things not profitable. Lord, forgive me for all those places I allow myself to go that are not worthy of You.*

This is how I sensed He responded:

> *I miss you when you let things silence My voice to you. I long to comfort, refresh and fill you continually. I am never too busy or preoccupied. My heart is filled with you. My heart holds you and all concerning you. My heart beats with a joy and inexpressible life I want to share with you. Your thoughts and concerns are already written there. I sift them through My hands and feel the very texture of them. There is nothing*

in front of you that I am not already completely familiar with. I know it all. Keep your eyes, mind and heart fully open to Me in everything so that I can join you in every detail of your life. It fills My heart to do it.

Would that rebuke, which reveals His longing for me, not draw me back to the heart of God? He didn't put me under shame and condemnation for wasting time with distractions. He may gently but firmly rebuke me, but I will still end up feeling valued by Him.

Again, the more we know the Bible, the more the Holy Spirit can quicken it to us in an experiential way and speak to our hearts. It is the personal word that is expressly for us in the moment, the *rhema**, where a verse may jump off the page and strike us deeply, bringing light and revelation that draws us to Christ.

---

* Footnote regarding our use of "logos" and "rhema:"
We understand that linguistically it is not totally accurate to make a rigid distinction between these two Greek words that refer to the "word". However, we believe that there is a very real difference between the impact of the written word of God (the Bible) which we may understand rationally, and those scriptures that the Holy Spirit highlights which impact our hearts. We have chosen to use the term "logos" for the written word of God and "rhema" for the words that the Holy Spirit speaks to our hearts personally, whether through highlighting a scripture or speaking to us directly.

Additional indicators

- His words are light, gentle and easily cut off by imposing our own thoughts or trying too hard to listen. As we trust Him to meet with us and speak to us in any way He chooses, we will always find Him faithful.
- When received, His words bring healing, freedom, transformation and strength to obey, even if it is costly.
- God's voice within us will not eradicate our personality or manner of speech. It may sound like us – our flavor – and so we are tempted to reject it. He is honoring our unique personality. In the same way, in the gospels, the Holy Spirit inspired four different men, each uniquely individual, to tell essentially the same story.

We hear people say, "The Lord told me" or "I heard the Lord" and so on. What do they mean? John Grace in *Hearing His Voice* says, "When God speaks to me in the Spirit, His voice translates itself into thought concepts that I can conceive in my mind. So, when I say, "I heard the Lord" or "The Lord spoke to me" I mean He spoke to me through a feeling in my spirit which translated into a thought in my mind ... It comes with a kind of rush and hits you as right."

The way God communicates may come as a picture or image in your mind. Jesus often spoke in parables and stories that created pictures to illustrate His teaching. Ask Him to open the "eyes of your heart" (Ephesians 1:18) to see things He may want to show you because a picture can simply express a thought that is more profound than a thousand words.

Several years ago, He reinforced my identity in Him in an amazing way, anchoring me (Diane) in the security of His

at will remain with me the rest of my life. I asked
, *how do You see me?*

,denly there was a picture of me as a little toddler
1air and He was holding me up on His breast and
wh... g loving words into my ears. He was dancing and
swaying with me. I heard this beautiful music, and I realized
that the music was His body moving through the air. Then I
asked: *Jesus, how do You see me?*

Immediately the picture changed, and I was a beautiful
bride dancing with a very handsome Jesus and He was
saying to me: "You are always going to be a bride. You are
never going to be a widow." You see He spoke to the place
in my heart where I lost my first husband as a result of the
Vietnam War and He knew I had that fear of being a widow
again. Then I asked: *Holy Spirit, how do You see me?*

At once, I saw myself in work overalls. For some reason
they were peppermint-striped. I have no idea why. And I had
a T-square and a hammer. Then I saw this huge figure next to
me where I could not see the head and face, in matching peppermint-striped overalls with a bigger T-square and hammer!

Of course, for each of us the Trinity will meet our hearts
in ways that are uniquely meaningful and helpful. For me,
those three pictures anchored my identity more than words
could express. I will always only be two years old and I have
a wonderful Daddy. Because I am in the bride (His church), I
will never be a widow. I am a co-worker and partner with the
Holy Spirit, and we are on the same mission.

Beyond a 'quiet time'

Do you look forward to and enjoy your time with Jesus?
Is it having "devotions" or devotion that motivates you in your
time with Him? Devotions can quickly become routine, legal,

boring and lifeless. If I'm not experiencing life with Him, I will not be able to remain expectant and confident in Him for the long haul.

Sharing my experience is not to suggest a formula or pattern but to encourage you to find the way to connect with God that is the most life-giving for you. It appears that too many exercise the discipline of a "quiet time" but don't feel like they really connect with God so they don't come away refreshed and strengthened. Maybe you feel your quiet time is too quiet. He has a way for you that you will look forward to and enjoy, and if you ask Him, He will help you find it.

Over the last 40 years, my time with God has changed as my relationship with the Lord has grown and developed. For me, it will not look the same every day. But my desire is always to connect with the heart of God.

Sadly, few Christians believe they can experience conversation and connection with God throughout their day, in the middle of their busyness. It is God's invitation to us all if we will purposely make a place for Him until it becomes a natural part of our daily lives.

God communicates with us in a multitude of ways, if we are attentive and discerning. As Henri Nouwen encourages us in *Discernment*, God speaks through nature, through people we encounter, through circumstances and through books we read.

Hearing God is not some practice that only excites those who are more contemplative or others who may be inclined to retreat from the world and have no desire to have an impact in it. God's invitation is as much to an accountant, a construction worker, a neurosurgeon or a homeschooling mom, as it is to a pastor.

Frank Laubach

Frank Laubach was a missionary in the 20th century known as the *Apostle to the Illiterates*. While working among Muslims in a remote location in the Philippines for over 40 years, told in his book *Forty Years with the Silent Billion*, he developed a literacy program that has reached an esti-mated 2.7 million people worldwide. This includes 150,000 Americans a year.

Author of numerous devotional writings, one of the most influential is *"The Game with Minutes."* He practiced and urged all believers to keep God in mind at least one second of every minute. Of course, we all fail, but then we can simply start again to turn our hearts and attention to Jesus, one minute at a time. One of my favorite quotes is Laubach's, in which he said: "All thought can become conversation with God." As this man lived his life among the poor, oppressed and illiterate, he made room to hear God and turn his heart to Him. As he ran his race out of this overflow, His legacy goes on impacting the world even today.

Preparing our hearts to listen

As I turn my heart to listen to the Father, my motivation is simply to encounter His heart in each area of my life. I want to always be listening with expectancy, so I can gain His perspective and have ongoing connection with Him throughout my day.

Focus

If we have not purposefully practiced tuning into the voice of God, we may not know how to become receptive to that still, small voice. So, my first step is to quiet myself before Him—what Graham Cooke calls *positioning myself within the*

heart of God. I make the choice by faith to turn to G
ask Him to help me focus.

We can't force ourselves to be inwardly still. The ı
we struggle, the more difficult it can become. The secret is
trusting Him to help us so that we can surrender, stop striving
and relax.

Position Your Heart

We "enter His gates with thanksgiving and His courts with
praise" (Psalm 100:4). I may thank Him for His desire to
speak to me. Declaring His kindness aloud helps my heart
to connect with Him and truly worship. Then, the joy of His
presence is often more powerfully experienced.

Also, whenever possible, read Scripture out loud, especially if you are struggling to connect with the Father. Take
those scriptures that reveal the love of the Father and rejoice
over them. Here are a couple of examples:

James 4:8 says: "Draw near to God and He will draw near
to you."

> *Father, I turn to You right now and I thank*
> *You that You are always ready and eager to*
> *meet with me.*

Or Matthew 11:28: "Come to Me, all who are weary and
heavy-laden and I will give you rest."

> *Jesus, I rejoice in Your invitation and I bring my*
> *anxious thoughts and burdens and lay them*
> *at Your feet. Thank You for being my place of*
> *refuge where I can let go, trust You with my*
> *concerns, relax on the inside and embrace the*
> *deep inward rest that You know I need.*

Distractions

Martha of Luke 10:41, was so focused and "distracted with all her preparations" that she missed the opportunity to heart connect with Jesus, the one she was intent on serving.

I am going to resist any interference or distraction. It's naïve for us to think that the most essential area of our life in our relationship with God is not going to be under attack from the enemy. I want to take authority over the accuser and silence Him in the mighty name of Jesus.

In quieting myself so I can focus, I may need to resist my flesh and my wandering thoughts. I may say, *No, I'm not going there right now.* I may write down things that I suddenly become aware of that need to be attended to and lay it aside so that I'm not carrying them in my mind.

I suggest you *gently reject* wandering thoughts. If I get frustrated with myself for not staying focused and being still, it exacerbates the distraction and hinders me from connecting with God. Gently yet firmly reject and turn your mind back to Him. Even this exercise alone will help strengthen your spirit.

I may ask Him about those distractions, making even these an opportunity to connect with Him: *Father, why do I keep going there? How can I cooperate with You, so I can be attentive to You?*

I may use sanctified imagination and ask: *Jesus, where are You right now?* If, with the eyes of my heart I see Him sitting next to me, waiting for me, I want to connect with Him. It helps me focus.

Confession

I may need to *confess* anything that is standing between God and I, and then let Him meet me at the point of my failure. I may journal what He speaks to me regarding my sin, as I shared earlier. As God appeals to His people: "'Come now, and let us reason together,' says the Lord, 'Though your sins are as scarlet they shall be white as snow'" (Isaiah 1:18).

Check out this verse which I was familiar with for many years but had missed something. "If we say that we have fellowship with Him yet walk in darkness, we lie ... if we walk in the light as He is in the light we have true unbroken fellowship with one another, [He with us and we with Him] and the blood of Jesus Christ His Son cleanses us from all sin and guilt" (1 John 1:6, 7, 9 – NASB, AMP). The 'true unbroken fellowship with one another,' in this context refers primarily, not to fellowship with other believers, but with God.

The enemy will use our sins and weaknesses to cause us to pull back from God. We usually view our need for confession of sin as a place of shame. So, often we are reluctant to admit our failure. We have largely lost touch with the power of confession in evangelical Christianity. Confession is the path to reconciliation and renewed fellowship. Bringing our failures to Jesus, instead of shrinking back, and openly confessing our sin to Him, is a wonderful opportunity to experience intimate connection with Him.

Or Simply

Sometimes I find I just need to cry out aloud: *Lord, I need You! Let me hear You!* I may pray in tongues which builds up my spirit (1 Corinthians 14:4). I'll do whatever it takes to focus my heart to listen.

A Listening Journal

I encourage you to use a journal, not to record your subjective thoughts and feelings but as a *Listening Journal*. You ask a question of God and because the Holy Spirit flows from within you have your pen ready and write the flow of whatever comes. Simply write until the flow stops. Don't worry about spelling or sentence structure. The flow of the Spirit is gentle and easily cut off when we try too hard. When finished, you can go back and check what you have heard against the litmus test and the filters we have given regarding His voice. Or, if needed, run it by a trusted and mature brother or sister.

I could ask a question like this many times and get a different answer:

Father, what do I need to know about You today that will help me trust You more? Or perhaps: *Father, how do You see me?*

About 11 years ago, we were enrolled in a Discipleship School at our church. At the same time, we were ministering to a girl who was in stage four cancer, Rick's brother was dying of cancer and our only daughter was preparing for her wedding and had moved back in with us. It was a very stressful time so that when I would sit down to try and have some focused connect time with God I just couldn't shift gears and connect with Him in a life-giving way. So, I asked: *Father, what do You have for my heart right now?* And He simply said: *I love you!* It just broke me. It broke the stress right off me. It shifted the atmosphere in a heartbeat. I spent the rest of my time receiving what He had said and rejoicing in it.

As we journal the flow that comes, the Holy Spirit will teach us to discern the difference between our rational thoughts and the spontaneous thoughts of God. As you journal, write down anything you receive, even if it is only one or two words. God often speaks simply but it is very profound, *if our hearts receive it*. Remember that by trying too hard and writing down your own reasoning, you can cut off the flow of the Holy Spirit. The Spirit's impressions can be slight and easily overcome. Just write the question and then write the flow of what comes.

After the flow stops, remember to go back and unpack what He says: *What is this going to look like in my life day-to-day? How do You want me to respond to this?* Then, write some more as the flow comes.

Not long ago I asked the Lord: *How do You see me today?* And He replied: *My little learner, still finding your way in Me.* There is so much to explore in the heart of God. We are all just beginners in life's greatest adventure.

Preparing Your Heart to Hear Him

Meeting God through listening to Him and journaling will probably be the most powerful tool for you to explore the heart of God and your relationship with Him.

In learning to listen to the Father's voice we suggest you:

- <u>Position your heart:</u> Turn off your phone. Limit external distractions (Matthew 6:6).
- <u>Focus</u>: Ask Him to help you quiet your heart to receive all He has.
- <u>Worship:</u> Praise Him for His desire to speak to you. We enter His gates with thanksgiving and expectancy (Psalm 100:4).
- <u>Resist</u> the enemy and he must flee (James 4:7). In Jesus' name, silence any voices not from Him. Ask for the covering of the blood of Jesus.
- <u>Confess</u> any sin you are aware of, journal what He says to you about it, then turn your heart to Him boldly and expectantly (Hebrew 10:19-22).
- <u>Distractions</u>: Write down any distractions to attend to later.
  If easily distracted, you may ask Him to help you "see" Him with you. Gently reject wandering thoughts. If

they persist, you may ask Him about what is on your mind and journal what He says.

- <u>Surrender</u>: We may think we know what God will say and simply listen to our own thoughts. Surrender your thoughts and desires so you can receive His.
  "I really want to hear what You have to say and not what I want to hear" – John Eldredge

As you yield your heart to Him, the spontaneous flow that comes from within you will usually be God speaking to you (John 7:38).

In the beginning, you may share your *Listening Journal* with a mentor or discipler for feedback and to make sure it lines up with Scripture.

ASK HIM AND JOURNAL

You can address Father, Jesus or the Holy Spirit.
Get ready to record first impressions.

Do I believe that You want to speak to me?

Why do You want to speak to me?

What do You want me to believe about hearing You?

<u>If you are having trouble receiving</u>, make these pronouncements in faith:

In the name of Jesus, I renounce the lie I cannot hear You.

I renounce the lie that You don't want to speak with me.

- <u>Sin</u>
  Clearly, un-confessed and habitual sin will erect a barrier between God and ourselves. Any refusal to acknowledge and repent for sin and rebellion, rather than coming to Him honestly with our struggles, addictions and failures, will keep Him from helping us.

- <u>Lack of Obedience</u>
  If He has already spoken clearly and we don't take it to heart or refuse to obey, then we cannot expect Him to speak to us further until we repent and respond.

- <u>An Unsurrendered Heart</u>
  If we are determined to guard our own desires and are not open to acting upon what He tells us, then we can't expect Him to speak. He may remain silent because of our rebellion. Check your heart before Him, but don't assume that if you can't hear anything that you are at fault. He may simply want you to sense His nearness and affection and enjoy being with Him.

- <u>Bitterness and Unforgiveness</u>
  If we have walls up with others, we will have walls up with God. As the Holy Spirit says: "The one who does not love his brother … cannot love God" (1 John 4:20). Refusing to surrender bitterness and forgive those who have wounded us, will keep our hearts hardened and unreceptive to the grace of God. Chapter 7 may be helpful here.

  Strong feelings or emotions in themselves are not a hindrance to hearing God or receiving from Him, *if* we are willing to bring them to Him in all honesty and process them with. He is not shockable! We may need to grieve pain, loss and disappointments that have resulted from wounds. Chapter 10 may be helpful here.

- An Undisciplined Mind

  Did you grow up on a diet of media or video games? Do you tend to keep yourself busy, even when you really don't need to? Many, if not most of us, have never cultivated inner stillness so we feel uneasy or restless when everything becomes quiet. The popularity of headphones and earplugs provide easy escape almost anywhere.

  "Be still and know that I am God" the Scripture beckons (Psalm 46:10 NKJV). We have not developed healthy internal boundaries and "closed the door" so we can connect with Jesus (Matthew 6:6). Restless minds are easily distracted so we are hindered from being sensitive to His speaking and find it difficult to stay focused and receive what He wants to communicate.

- Fear of Silence

  We all long to be met in the silence, but the fear of being alone in the silence can keep us from going there. We often fill silence with noise which keeps us from finding the intimacy we long for. We go to the beach or the forest, but all too often are met with the boom box that drowns out the music of nature and the God who orchestrated it to draw us to Himself.

- A Polluted Mind

  If we have allowed our minds to become polluted through dwelling on things that are not true, right, pure, lovely ... (Philippians 4:8) then the enemy will

have plenty of ammunition to distract us and draw us away from God. Our thought patterns cultivate pathways in the brain that make it difficult to break free from, although, with the Spirit's help, we can develop healthy pathways to which we naturally gravitate.

- ## False Comfort
  In our desire for comfort, assurance and security, if we have cultivated the habit of gravitating to social media instead of turning to Jesus as our source, we will not have developed any expectancy that He can speak to our hearts and fulfill us when we do listen. Especially if we are excessively extroverted, we may be prone to please others rather than be a friend of God. So, instead of giving Him our attention when He wants to speak to us, we feel obligated to immediately respond to that text. Of course, there are other false comforts like entertainment, food or keeping ourselves busy.

- ## Analytical Control
  If we are excessively proud of our intellect and reasoning ability, leaning on our own understanding (Proverbs 3:5), we will never grow to trust God.
  We are invited to come to God as a child, humble ourselves, surrender control, acknowledge that our understanding is relatively miniscule and ask Him to enlighten us.

- ## Presumption
  As we are trying to hear God, it is easy to assume what we think He is going to say to us, and so we listen to our own thoughts instead of His. Again, recognizing our total limitation, we must simply surrender

our opinions and ideas, and invite God to speak what He alone knows we need to hear.

Filters in Hearing

We may be hearing God, but filter what we hear.

- <u>Idols in the Heart</u>
  If we grasp onto our preferences or what we think are our rights, they easily become our idols that come between us and God. As a result, we will find ourselves praying through that idol to God, and we hear back through that idol what we want to hear.

  We so want that girl or that job that we fix our hearts on, instead of saying, *Lord I yield this to You, and if this is what is best for my heart and life in You, then I trust You to give it back to me.* We are warned in Psalm 106:14-15 (AMP): "[They] lusted exceedingly in the wilderness and tempted and tried to restrain God with their insistent desires in the desert. And He gave them their request but sent leanness into their souls."

  To hear Him clearly, we must surrender our strong preferences and desires to Him and trust Him to give us what our hearts truly need. He warns us: "I will speak to this people, and even so they will not listen to Me" (1 Corinthians 14:21). Still, we don't want to minimize the difficulty and cost that can be required to surrender the desires of our heart and trust God to fully meet us, no matter the outcome.

- <u>Fear of Deception</u>
  We are unable to receive what God has to say because we are afraid that we are making this up in our own mind, deluding ourselves or being misled. We are not trusting God to help us in our weakness and feel we must protect ourselves. As He said to Rick: *Your caution was fear masquerading as wisdom.* If we are unsure if what we are hearing is from God, whether it is internally in our own thoughts or whether we are listening to a preacher, we are encouraged to "Test the spirits to see whether they are from God" (1 John 4:1).

  Jesus said: "When the Helper comes, whom I will send to you from the Father, that is the Spirit of truth, who proceeds from the Father, He will bear witness of Me" (John 15:26). And again, referring to the Holy Spirit: "His anointing teaches you about all things, and is true and is not a lie" (1 John 2:27). We can also check with the guidelines in Chapter 4. Does it draw us to Jesus and line up with Scripture?

- <u>Impure Motives</u>
  We listen with the intention of correcting others or to prove a point, validate our position or defend our choices.

The Pregnant Silence of God

What about the apparent silence of God—those times when we are just not hearing anything? We may feel frustrated and discouraged or we may feel pressure to try and make something happen. I have found that if I have consistently and with expectancy practiced quieting my heart and hearing His voice, then in times of apparent silence I will be able to experience what I call the *pregnant silence* of God. This is the tangible presence of God that goes beyond words. I'm sure that He is with me and for me, and I can rest in the confidence that He is meeting me, whether I hear anything or not.

> *Am I seeking the voice of God*
> *or seeking God Himself?*

Author Linda Wagner advises: *Don't force yourself to hear. If there is silence, be still and know that He is God whether or not you 'feel' or 'hear' Him. (Learning to Listen to God,* p. 53)

This silence will not be a void that makes me anxious, but where I know God is ministering to my spirit. It's like being in a room with a lover where there is no need for words. In my experience, this most often happens in the times when I feel the most depleted. In faith and trust, as we quietly sit before Him, He is able to pour into us His peace and refreshment, and the comforting assurance that He is holding onto us. And, more than this,

> *it brings delight to the heart of God that*
> *we simply want to be with Him and not*
> *require anything of Him.*

❈

ASK HIM AND JOURNAL

"My heart has heard You say, 'Come and talk with Me.' And my heart responds, 'Lord I am coming'" (Psalm 27:8).

"Listen carefully to Me and eat what is good. And delight yourself in abundance" (Isaiah 55:2b).

Turn your heart to Him and ask Him to speak and to help you by faith hear the flow of the Spirit as He speaks to you. Let Him tell you, as no one sees himself clearly.

Do not analyze as you write.

Once you have received, go back and prayerfully read it.

Father, what things have I chosen that have hindered me from hearing You?

What do You have to say about any filters I have used in listening to You?

Father, what idols have I held in my heart that would filter what I hear from You?

How do You want me to respond to this?

CHAPTER 6

Freedom from Lies

*W*e are created for intimacy with God, but we have an enemy and he knows that God wants this more than anything else. Therefore, Satan's primary goal, the objective of all his attacks, is simply to prevent or kill intimacy. The way he does that is to convince us to believe his lies. Jesus calls him "the father of lies" (John 8:44). All lies originate from Satan. In fact, the enemy, in every Old Testament reference bar one (1 Chronicles 21:1) is literally called, not Satan, but the accuser.

I have never found any exception to the fact that no matter what difficulty of the heart we are struggling to overcome—what addictions or destructive behavior we wrestle with, whether the result of fear, anger, depression, passivity, loneliness, hopelessness … you name it, that underneath it all, the deepest root of all our issues boils down to lies we believe.

These foundational lies are stunningly simple—either lies about God or lies about ourselves, and typically a combination of both. Essentially, they are lies we believe about the character of God and lies we believe about our true identity in Christ.

In a nutshell:

> *God can't be trusted.*
> *There is something wrong with me.*

If we believe either of these lies it will hinder, if not kill, intimacy. The accuser doesn't need to be any more creative because these lies are so effective, and we buy into his deception all too easily.

At the very beginning of Jesus' ministry and again on the cross, we clearly see the focus of the enemy's attacks. At Jesus' baptism, the Father said: "This is My beloved Son in who I am well pleased" (Luke 3:22). In effect, the Father declared: *This is Your identity and this is My heart for You.*

Next, Jesus was led by the Spirit into the wilderness where He was tempted. Jesus was hungry, and the devil said: "*If You are the Son of God*, tell this stone to become bread" (Luke 4:3; emphasis added), immediately questioning the very identity the Father had spoken over Him. Moreover, the devil was calling into question the trustworthiness of Jesus' Father.

When Jesus was on the cross, the accuser hurled abuse at Him through the religious leaders: "'*If You are the Son of God*, come down from the cross.' The chief priests, along with the scribes and elders mocked Him saying: He trusts in God; let Him deliver Him now, *if He takes pleasure in Him;* for He said, 'I am the Son of God'" (Matthew 27:39-43; emphasis added). The enemy knew that if he could get Jesus to doubt the love of His Father or His identity as His Son, the whole redemptive plan would unravel. The enemy attacks us the same way.

John the apostle, succinctly declares in 1 John 5:19, 20 the provision in Jesus which fortifies us against the accuser's two-fold attack. "We know that we are of God and the whole world lies in the power of the evil one. And we know that the Son of God has come and has given us understanding in order that we might *know Him who is true* [the true character of the Father], and *we are in Him* who is true, in His Son Jesus Christ [our true identity]" (emphasis added).

So, we see how the enemy seeks to kill intimacy with God. Jesus, knowing we would face the same strategy as He did, overcame to pave the way for us so we, too, can thrive in our relationship with the Father, come what may. As you continue to read, you will find simple, biblical ways to overcome and grow in your confidence and joy in God.

> *What comes into our mind when we think about God is the most important thing about us.*

Were we able to extract from any man a complete answer to the question, "What comes into your mind when you think about God?" we might predict with certainty the spiritual future of that man.

A.W. Tozer

What we think God is like will determine the relationship we have with God. Our thoughts about God will determine not only who we are but how we live.
The Good and Beautiful God: Falling in love with the God Jesus knows (p.88).

James Bryan Smith

Jesus said in two commandments depend the whole law and the prophets: "You shall love the Lord your God with

61:3 ᴋᴊᴠ). Sometimes we just feel heavy, discouraged and weighed down like we have a piano on our back, though we may not know specifically why. We need to be aware that the enemy will use pressures and fears that seem very legitimate and understandable so that we come to accept them as normal, but he accentuates and magnifies them to "wear down the saints" (Daniel 7:25) and bring us into bondage.

What about the "spirit of fear" (2 Timothy 1:7 ᴋᴊᴠ). There are lots of fears that can be totally legitimate: the fear of losing control of your car on an icy road. But there are times when we are not in crisis, yet we are uptight, anxious, stressed out and we don't know why. Or, the fear is totally out of proportion. Or, the fear controls us and has power over us–like the fear of committing to relationships, irrational fears and panic attacks. Something deeper is moving us then. We need to be aware of the enemy's tactics if we are to deny him access to our hearts.

We will address overcoming spiritual strongholds in Chapter 8, following Forgiveness.

Common source of lies

It is staggering how horrendous events may not scar the hearts of some people deeply, whereas for others the slightest event can leave deep scars that result in lasting pain and brokenness.

One young woman with deep-seated inhibition and self-consciousness was having a conversation with the Father when He reminded her of a memory as a 3-year-old where she walked into a room of adults who suddenly became silent as she entered. Her perception as a child was that they were talking about her negatively and they didn't want her to hear it. The little girl concluded that there was something wrong with her.

It was not until she was sharing this memory with her mother as an adult, that her mother pointed out that the adults had been preparing a surprise birthday party for her the next day. Because of the lie she believed as a 3-year-old, this young woman had been painfully self-conscious and struggled with recurring feelings of worthlessness for decades. She was bound by lies that came from a wound that was entirely unintended, but nevertheless, devastating.

Just as flies sow maggots in open wounds, so the accuser sows his corrupting lies in our heart wounds. These lies are sown especially when we are young, through wounding experiences that most often involve authority figures, particularly parents, but also coaches, teachers and preachers, as well as siblings and peers at school. The enemy capitalizes on pain and rejection to accuse God.

For example, say your dad was caught up with his work and he never connected with you emotionally. The accuser may then tell you that you can't trust God to take care of you either. *Father God is not dependable. He's emotionally distant. He doesn't care about your pain.* Or, the enemy may accuse you. *The reason your dad didn't spend time with you is that you are really not worth it. You are not valued. You are not significant.*

Or, perhaps you were in elementary school and your teacher humiliated you in front of the class because you failed a test. The accuser may move in and say: *Don't get vulnerable with God. Don't take a risk with Him and get too close to Him. He'll expose your weakness.* Or, the enemy may accuse you: *You're a loser! You have to perform to be accepted. You have to protect yourself because no-one else will.*

Father, what is the truth I need to know about You in exchange for this lie?

> Unpack by asking further questions if necessary, so it is clearly understood. Declare it and rejoice until it resonates in your heart.

Father, is there any lie I believe about myself? List any He reveals.

How has this lie affected my relationship with You?

How has this lie affected my relationship with others?

Father, am I willing to renounce this lie?

If yes, *I renounce the lie that I ...*

If not, then Chapter 14 on *Self-Hatred* may be helpful.

I repent for giving the lie influence and authority. Ask for and receive forgiveness.

―――――――――――――

Footnote:

It's clear from Scripture that God is ready to forgive (Psalm 86:5) and promises to those who confess their sin that He is faithful and just to forgive their sin and cleanse them from all unrighteousness (1 John 1:9). It is especially powerful when someone receives a personal, spoken word that confirms it in their hearts.

If someone doesn't hear from the Lord, then they can rest in the assurance of the written word. Perhaps you can ask: Father, is there a lie I believe about You or myself that keeps me from hearing You say I am forgiven, according to Your written word?

Unpack by asking additional questions if necessary, so it is clearly understood. Declare it and rejoice until it resonates in your heart.

GOING DEEPER

The Power of the Cross of Christ
Demonstrating the truth that demolishes the lies hindering intimacy with God.

John the Baptist exhorts us twice to "Behold the Lamb of God," the one whom God would sacrifice for our sin (John 1:29, 36).

To "behold" means "to look earnestly, intently." The writer to the Hebrews exhorts us to fix our eyes on Jesus ... who endured the cross (Hebrews 12:2). In other words, let the eyes of your heart stay there. Take it in.

Paul said to the Corinthian church: "I determined to know nothing among you except Jesus Christ and Him crucified" (1 Corinthians 2:2).

What Jesus accomplished on the cross is so profound we will never in this life plumb its depths. However, there is one aspect I want to draw your attention to that can be very helpful when it comes to overcoming lies.

Jesus, speaking of His crucifixion, said: "As Moses lifted up the serpent in the wilderness, even so must the Son of Man be lifted up" (John 3:14). In Numbers 21 we find "The people spoke against God ... and the Lord sent fiery serpents among the people and they bit the people so that many people of Israel died" (5, 6). The people repented, and the Lord said to Moses to make a serpent and put it on a standard ... and everyone who is bitten, "when he looks at it, he shall live" (8).

In other words, when anyone looked at the bronze serpent on the pole they were delivered from the serpent's poison. Here is a clear illustration of the power of the cross of our Lord Jesus–if we really see it!

The enemy's poison, his lies, the fiery darts (Ephesians 6:16), are targeted to undermine our intimacy with God. Essentially, these lies always call into question the character of God or our identity in Christ, or both. If we believe these lies and take in his poison, our intimacy with God will be compromised, if not destroyed.

We cannot enjoy intimacy with the Father if we doubt His love for us or our value to Him. That's one reason why the Father made the cross so pivotal in the great story of redemption, knowing exactly how the enemy was going to assault us.

To demolish the first lie that God doesn't really care about us, the cross of Christ is the clearest demonstration imaginable of the depth of the Father's love for us and the strength of His passion to bring us to Himself–that He would sacrifice His only son, His dearest companion, so that we would have a way to receive cleansing and forgiveness and come confidently into fellowship with Him.

Secondly, any doubts we have of our value to God are forever removed when we take to heart the fact that He could have paid no higher price for us.

Fixing the gaze of our hearts on Jesus who willingly laid down His life for us–to meditate on the incredible truth of the Father's love and of His desire for us so vividly displayed in the cross–delivers us from the poisonous lies of the enemy, scattering confusion, demolishing fear, and lifting heaviness so we can enjoy the intimacy which the Father so dearly paid for.

What better focus for listening and journaling than the cross! Let us invite God to delve beneath our superficial understanding and penetrate our hearts with the truth of all He accomplished for us on the cross that dynamically sets us free to grow in our knowledge and enjoyment of Him.

Ask Jesus:

What question do You want me to ask You about the cross?

What truth about You or myself do I need to know here?

Then, as He shares His heart with you– Journal it. Declare it. Rejoice in it. Digest it. Receive it!

CHAPTER 7

Forgiving for Heart Wounds

*E*ven though we live in a city, Diane and I are very thankful to live in a home where we overlook a ravine filled with trees, so squirrels and birds are our welcome guests. Among the most beautiful birds attracted to our bird feeders are the cardinals, gorgeous in their scarlet plumage. Recently, a juvenile male cardinal, still brown-feathered and barely beginning to show his mature color, came to our window sill and began vigorously pecking the window. Day after day he returned and persisted. I was surprised he didn't get punch drunk and give up. We had seen this behavior by male cardinals at our previous home and assume they are attacking their reflection in an attempt to defend their territory. So, here is this bird, devoting his attention and expending all this energy in an attempt to do something that was understandable but utterly futile.

How often do we find ourselves, reacting to perceived or even very real threats, with thoughts and behavior that serve only to knock ourselves about? Unforgiveness is the next best thing to banging our heads against a brick wall. In our attempt to attack or defend, we are the ones getting beaten up. Heartfelt forgiveness for the wounds to our hearts is indispensable if we are to become whole.

The key to freedom

As we have said, a wound is, most often, the seedbed of lies which hinder intimacy with God. Frequently, when we are wounded, we begin to believe lies about God or ourselves. Unless we forgive the one who caused the wound, we will never be free from the lies rooted there.

Harboring bitterness and unforgiveness is one of the greatest barriers to us enjoying intimacy with God. As 1 John 4:20 says: "The one who does not love his brother, cannot love God."

If we refuse to forgive, the enemy is given an open door to reinforce those lies, frequently born in childhood, and bring us into deeper bondage. For example, if I was unjustly ill-treated but began to believe the lie that I deserved it, then I may anticipate further ill treatment which the enemy will gladly seek to support through ongoing negative circum-stances. Here lies the power of forgiveness which is a vital and potent key to releasing the stronghold of the lies and bring healing to the heart.

In Matthew 18:29-35 we read, "… you wicked slave, I for-gave you all that debt because you pleaded with me. Should you not also have had mercy on your fellow slave …? And his lord … handed him over to the torturers until he should repay … forgive from your heart." Here is a vivid example of how a bitter root causes damage and continues to defile subsequent relationships and events because we have not released our unforgiveness. Unforgiveness will keep us in bondage because we move out from under the protection of God and we put ourselves in the power of the enemy allowing him to reinforce the lie in that wound again and again. *I am worthless. God cannot be trusted.* This is an example of what it means to be "handed over to the torturers" and tormentors.

The enemy will orchestrate circumstances again and again to re-echo that original wounding event and reinforce the lies that were born in it.

A young man came to me (Rick) who was struggling with sudden feelings of revulsion toward his fiancée, and he was only six weeks out from the wedding. As we asked the Father to reveal the root of the matter, it became clear that this young man was harboring deep bitterness toward his mother whom he felt had always tried to control and manipulate him. From this place of wounding, he came to believe that he was weak and did not have what it takes to be a good husband.

As much as he tried to love his beautiful fiancée, he was unable to overcome these strong feelings that he should avoid her and not allow himself to be vulnerable with her for fear she would take advantage of him. At first, he simply would not forgive his mother, until he realized that his bitterness was poisoning his attitude toward his fiancée. It was only when he forgave his mother for leading him to feel that he was worthless and a pushover and repented for closing his heart to his mother and for his judgment of her, that he was able to receive new love and appreciation for his fiancée. He was then also able to receive fresh identity from the Father of his value as a man.

We must come to the place where we will not allow the wounds of others to define us. Whether you were wounded by your father or mother, whether you were victimized, or whether you have been intentionally and purposefully sinned against, none of these wounds define you. We are defined by who God says we are, not by the treatment of others!

However, it's only when we forgive that we can be set free from the power of the lies born in that wound. It cuts off the enemy's right to traffic with us and then the lie can freely be renounced. Forgiveness sets our heart free from the power of the wound, so we can move forward to receive the truth from God and have it really sink into our hearts.

Clearly, we may need to forgive for an offense or wound that has not led to any lies we believe. For example, my wife may have made a comment that wounded me, and I could be tempted to hold a grudge. Simply and genuinely forgiving her may be all that is needed. If I find myself more deeply offended, then it may be helpful to ask the Father why, and I may discover there is a lie I believe that was reinforced by my wife's comment, which I should address. But, if we simply need to forgive, a journaling exercise is given following *Steps to Forgiveness*.

Forgiveness involves four parts:
1. The injury to us, and the debt incurred as a result.
2. Cancelling that debt by releasing the offender from the debt we feel they owe us.
3. Absolving the offender, where we don't require anything of them to put it right. We set them free them from the responsibility to meet our need. They are absolved, regardless of their response.
4. Being willing, by the grace of God, to live with the consequences of another's sin. His grace is abundantly available for us here.

To forgive is to choose to move over in our hearts and no longer give power to those who have wounded us. Often it is not easy to forgive, but God, who Himself is ready to forgive (Psalm 86:5) will gladly help us release our offenders.

Forgiving for the heart wound

> *It is not the wound itself, but our sinful reactions to the wound that give the enemy the right of access to traffic with us and establish strongholds in our lives.*

It is not the wound itself, but what we do with it.

Stacy Eldredge in *Captivating* calls it the 'unholy alliance' and says: "The only thing more tragic than the things that have happened to us is what we have done with them. Words were said. Painful words. Things were done. Awful things. And they shaped us. Something inside us shifted. *We embraced the message of our wounds.* We accepted a twisted view of ourselves. We chose a way of relating to our world, and a way of viewing God and relating to God."

Too often, we forgive only for the outward act, what was done to us, the actions of the offender, and wonder why we don't experience more freedom. But the wounds that have far greater impact, that can last a lifetime, are what we chose to believe as a result of the wound, "the message of our wounds", often the lies we believe about God or ourselves.

> *Many believers have forgiven numerous times with little effect because they have not recognized the vital difference between forgiving for what was done to them and forgiving for what they were led to believe as a result!*

We can ask God to show us the impact on our heart as a result of a wound, what we believed or felt as a consequence. What He reveals may come as a surprise, but it rings true. Then, we may need to ask Him for help to forgive for the heart wound. Forgiveness for the heart wound opens the door for much deeper healing, transformation and intimacy with God.

For example, I may forgive my dad for being emotionally disconnected and absent–what he did. But then I can ask the Holy Spirit to tell me how this impacted my heart and what it is that I need to forgive dad for. I may need to forgive him for leading me to feel insignificant, unimportant and alone. I may also need to forgive him for leading me to believe that God would treat me the same way, that He too is emotionally disconnected, doesn't really care and cannot be depended upon for encouragement and help when I need it.

Forgiveness is a choice

As believers we are commanded to forgive. We don't have to feel forgiving to forgive. It is a choice. If I forgive someone a debt, I can simply choose to tear up the bill and release them from any obligation to repay. I don't have to be emotional about it for it to be effective. But I do have to forgive from the heart (Matthew 18:35).

A young man who was about to head overseas to the mission field was struggling with depression. His father also suffered from depression as did his father's father. Years of counseling had confirmed to him that there was a generational bondage that required him to forgive his father. Many times, he had said the words, *Father, I forgive my dad*, but there had been no substantial change in his condition.

I encouraged him to ask the Father whether he was willing to forgive his dad for the heart wounds he had received–his passivity, negativity and anger, and his failure to initiate and seek to understand him, which had led him to feel insecure, fearful and of no value. He heard, *No, you are not!*

It became obvious that he had been going through the motions of forgiveness but had not forgiven from his heart, as Jesus made clear was essential. When he had asked the Father what his life would be like if he didn't forgive from the heart, he was told his depression would continue. The Father even told him he would be free of depression if he truly forgave his dad, and still he was unwilling to relinquish his bitterness and anger. It was only after he asked the Father how he saw his dad that he began to see his father as a little boy being abused by his father. That was the insight he needed to finally be willing to forgive from his heart and begin to find substantial freedom from depression.

Here again, we see how critical it is for us to ask the Father to search our hearts and not assume we know, for He alone sees us clearly.

Why are we reluctant to forgive?

1. It could be an unacknowledged need. We think we have already forgiven. We've moved on. We don't dwell on it any more. But, we may not be in touch with the hidden wound and the pain and resentment that is there. As adults, we tend to minimize, in particular, the wounds we received in childhood. *It wasn't that big a deal. I was just a kid and I didn't understand.* The fact is, that I have to deal with what I got as a child, whether my perception was accurate or not, because that is what the enemy works with.

2. Denial. We have not wanted to acknowledge the sins against us by those whom we have wanted to love us. Or, we don't want to dishonor or seem ungrateful, especially to parents, by admitting the need to forgive

them. Actually, forgiving and blessing parents is honoring them.

3. We accept all the blame. We excuse the sin of others, minimize it and we conclude it's our fault. This is often the case with children who have been sexually abused, or women who have been raped, who believe the lie that it was their fault, that there was something wrong with them.

4. Because of our own guilt, we feel the need to blame. A guy who takes advantage of a girl sexually may blame her for leading him on. We blame to feel justified. It's like guilt and blame are on either side of balancing scales. We have guilt about the way we have treated someone on one side. But on the other side, we can balance our guilt by blaming the offender and holding onto our anger toward them. If we were to forgive them for the way they offended us and let our anger go, then our blame would be removed from the scale. But then, because of our bad behavior, our guilt level will rise, and we will have to face it. So, to self-protect, we hold onto blame in an attempt to justify our guilt. This is often the case where there is mutual unforgiveness, such as in a marriage or a parent-child relationship.

5. It is asking a great deal to expect a person who has been truly victimized and sinned against, to forgive their violator. We may feel that by forgiving we are agreeing that what happened was not that significant, that the sin of the offender was not that bad. It seems that to forgive is to minimize it. But while we may forgive the person who sinned against us, they will still have to answer to God for their sin.

6. Ungodly justice or revenge. We want to punish our offender by holding onto unforgiveness and letting them know how much they have hurt us by not forgiving them and withholding our love. But this means that we remain anchored to what they did to us, giving the person power to continue to hurt us. We think we are protecting ourselves from being hurt again by withdrawing, hardening our hearts and distancing ourselves. In fact, we are not only building walls against the offender, it creates walls between ourselves and God.

7. We may not want to forgive because we take up an offense for someone else. We may be tempted to believe that our unforgiveness is justified because we feel it is motivated by our concern for the one who was hurt.

Help to Forgive

When we have difficulty forgiving an offender, one of the best things to do is to ask the Father how He sees that person. Often, but of course not always, the hurtful actions of the offender spring from their own wounding, as we illustrated earlier in this chapter. Hence, the wounds they inflict say more about the brokenness of their own hearts than reflect on the person they have wounded. If my parents were not loved, they may well have struggled to know how to love.

When it comes to actual intended abuse, we must acknowledge that this was sin against us. We must name it for what it is–and then extend forgiveness. We must specifically name the sin and the offender. We must call it what it is and bring it into the light. With our confession of those specific sins and the abuse against us, and by forgiving the abuser, only then are we able to be healed from the wound and freed from the lies born in that abuse.

For some, if not many, there are areas of unresolved grief or loss, where you forgive again and again in the same area with no relief. The pain from the wound does not go away, which can lead to retreating into self-protection, hardening of the heart, lingering sadness or even despair and depression. We will address how to process grief and loss with the Father in Chapter 10.

How do we stay in forgiveness?

We may have forgiven, but with time we may recognize that the negative impact of the offender's actions on our life is far greater than we first thought. Or, we may continue to be impacted by the unchanged life of the offender. Peter must have thought he was impressing Jesus when he suggested forgiving seven times. Jesus knew we would have to forgive frequently so He set no limits (Matthew 18:22). This doesn't necessarily mean we haven't forgiven the first time. It may simply mean we need to forgive from a deeper place (a heart wound). If we continue to forgive in intolerable circumstances and choose not to go with any sinful reaction, we will increasingly become free to receive the grace of God and overcome the tactics of the enemy to keep us bound to those who have wounded us.

Possible Indications of Unforgiveness

Ask the Holy Spirit to reveal to you if there are any indications of these in your life.

Depression	Hurt feelings
Anger	Ungratefulness
Cynicism	Negative expectation
Mistrust	Cannot receive correction
Defensiveness	Justifying yourself
Judgment and Criticism	Pride, self-righteousness
Obsessive thinking	Thoughts of revenge
Insensitivity	Excessive need of approval
Tension around others (uncomfortable, avoiding)	Self-condemnation

How do we know we have forgiven?

- We are able to experience compassion or acceptance of our offender's woundedness - as Jesus did: "Father forgive them for they know not what they do ..." (Luke 23:24)
- We are able to accept those we have forgiven without the need to change them.
- We are able to find release from the power of the emotion over the wound.
- Negative feelings will continue to diminish or go away entirely as we consistently choose to forgive whenever those feelings arise.
- We are able to move towards forgiveness more quickly when offended again.

The following diagram illustrates the critical role of forgiveness in the process of renouncing lies and receiving the truth about God and ourselves.

Overcoming Wounds and Lies to Restore Intimacy with God

THE BATTLE OVER INTIMACY

- The enemy's strategy is to kill our intimacy with the Lord by speaking lies against the character of God or our value/identity in Christ (Matthew 27:43).
- We believe lies in our hearts (Romans 10:10) but are often desensitized to the lies.
- God alone knows our hearts. We ask the wonderful Counselor to reveal lies (Isaiah 9:6).
- Lies are mostly sown in wounds. We must forgive the offender to break the power of the lie born there.

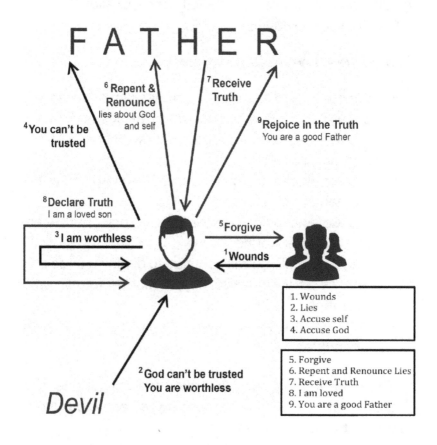

F A T H E R

[6] Repent & Renounce lies about God and self

[7] Receive Truth

[4] You can't be trusted

[9] Rejoice in the Truth You are a good Father

[8] Declare Truth I am a loved son

[5] Forgive

[3] I am worthless

[1] Wounds

[2] God can't be trusted You are worthless

Devil

1. Wounds
2. Lies
3. Accuse self
4. Accuse God

5. Forgive
6. Repent and Renounce Lies
7. Receive Truth
8. I am loved
9. You are a good Father

Diagram Sequence

1. 'Joe' is wounded.
2. Enemy accuses Joe and God.
3. If Joe reacts badly, he agrees with the enemy and partners with him. Joe condemns himself: *I am worthless.*
4. He accuses God: *You can't be trusted.*
5. If he responds as he should, then Joe forgives those who hurt him.
6. He repents to the Father and renounces those lies about God and himself.
7. Joe turns to the Father to hear what He has to say about Himself, His heart for Joe, and about Joe's true identity in Christ.
8. Joe rejoices in his true identity, declaring it over himself. *I am a loved son!*
9. Joe rejoices in the truth of who God really is. *You are a good Father!*

To do this can be life-changing!

FREEDOM FROM LIES THROUGH FORGIVENESS

- **Forgive** whoever wounded us that led to believing any lies.
- **Renounce** lies about God or ourselves.
- **Repent** for partnering with the enemy and for giving those lies authority.
- **Receive** from God the truth that will ignite our hearts to replace the lies believed there.
  To receive, we must first yield and make room in our hearts to embrace what God says.
  Unpack with God what He says by asking Him more questions until it is practical and helpful.

- Then declare and **Rejoice** in the truth until our hearts are full!

This way, our minds are renewed and our hearts strengthened so we can both recognize and resist lies, temptations and hindrances to enjoying intimacy with the Father.

ASK HIM AND JOURNAL on Forgiveness and Wounds Involving Lies.

Don't rush this. Make sure your heart is engaged. This will help set you free from the lies of the enemy and enable you to receive, perhaps as never before, the heart of the Father and your identity in Him.

You may want to refer to the lies you have journaled in the previous chapter.

If so, then return to *Steps to Forgiveness and Healing* beginning with the *Origin of the Lie.*

Steps to Forgiveness and Healing

Lies which hinder our intimacy with God are mostly born in wounds.
We must forgive the offender to break the power of the lie.
Often, after discovering a distorted view of God or self, we may ask:

FIND THE LIE
- Father, what lie do I believe (about You or myself) here?

ORIGIN OF LIE
- Father, when did I first begin to believe this lie?

FORGIVE, RELEASE & BLESS
- *Father, who do I need to forgive who led me to believe this lie? What do I need to forgive ___ for?* (Forgive for heart wound, not just outward act)
- *Am I willing to forgive___?* (If not) *If I do forgive ___ what will my life be like? If I don't forgive ___what will my life be like?*
- *Father, I forgive ___ for ___ and for leading me to feel ___.* (Repeat as many times as needed) *Is there anything else I need to forgive __ for in this area?*
- (Optional) *Father, show me Jesus on the cross.* Then: *Father I take their sins against me and the wounds I received and lay them upon the body of Jesus on the cross. Jesus, I thank You that You carried all my pain and sorrow* (Isaiah 53:4-5) *so I don't need to carry them anymore.*
- *I release ___ from all their offenses and wounds against me. I bless them in Jesus' name.*
- *I repent for my sinful reactions, any bitterness, resentment or anger I have had toward my offender. Father, do You forgive me?* (Yes) *Then I forgive myself.*

RENOUNCE
- *Father, I renounce the lie that You __* (Corresponding lies about God and self)

REPENT
- *Father, forgive me for partnering with the enemy and believing these lies* (Be explicit) *about You (and about myself).*

95

- *Father, do You forgive me? (Yes*) Then I receive Your forgiveness and forgive myself.*

RECEIVE!

- *Father, what truth do You have for my heart in exchange for these lies?* Unpack with Him by asking more questions until it is practical and helpful.

REJOICE!

- Thank Him, declaring and receiving the truth in your heart.

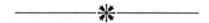

ASK HIM AND JOURNAL on Forgiveness *Not* Involving Lies

Father what do You have to say to me about unforgiveness in my life right now?

Father, how has unforgiveness in my life affected my heart interaction with You?

Father, why do You want me to be free of this?

Father, is there anyone against whom I am holding unforgiveness?

---

*Footnote:
It's clear from Scripture that God is ready to forgive (Psalm 86:5) and promises to those who confess their sin that He is faithful and just to forgive us (1 John 1:9). It is especially powerful when someone receives a personal, spoken word that confirms it in their hearts.

- *What do I need to forgive ___ for?*
    (Forgive for heart wound, not just outward act)
- *Am I willing to forgive___? (If not) If I do forgive ___ what will my life be like?*
    If I don't forgive ___what will my life be like?
- *Father, I forgive ___ for ___ and for leading me to feel ___.*
    (Repeat as many times as needed)
    is there anything else I need to forgive ___ for in this area?
- *I release ___ from all their offenses and wounds against me. I bless them in Jesus' name.*
- *I repent for my sinful reactions, any bitterness, resentment or anger I have had towards ___. Father, do You forgive me? (Yes) Then I forgive myself.*
- *Father, how do You see ___? How do You want me to respond to them?*

CHAPTER 8

Demolishing Spiritual Strongholds

*T*he enemy gains access to our hearts through our sinful choices. Therefore, it is necessary to deal with the ground we have given him to remove his legal right of entry. To overlook this is to leave the door open for the enemy to return.

In Chapter 6, we addressed the need to renounce and repent for believing lies of God and ourselves and receive the truth in our hearts. Because lies are nearly always born in wounds, in Chapter 7 we pointed out the absolute necessity of forgiving those who have wounded us, if we are to enjoy freedom from those lies.

What do we do if we have renounced lies, repented, forgiven as the Lord has revealed the need, and we still find ourselves harassed by those lies and stuck in old, negative behavioral patterns? What do we do if we are making little headway despite our best efforts to take thoughts captive, stand in the truth of what the Lord has spoken, and keep our hearts free from any bitterness and resentment?

> *Whenever we find sinful patterns that are beyond our willpower to break, we may ask God whether we have opened a door that has allowed a demonic stronghold to be established.*

Towards the end of Chapter 6, we introduced the possibility of demonic spirits and their role in keeping us from enjoying intimacy with God.

At the end of this chapter we have a simple Renunciation that can help guide you through the process of partnering with God to bring down these strongholds. Let us never forget that, in ourselves, we are powerless to deal with the enemy. But, once we have done the critical work of denying the accuser his right of access through repentance and forgiveness, we can confidently claim our authority in Christ and remove any stronghold. So, what authority to deal with strongholds have we been given in Christ?

Jesus said: "Behold I have given you authority … over all the power of the enemy" (Luke 10:19). "And these signs will accompany those who have believed: in My name they will cast out demons" (Mark 16:17).

Some Guidelines

While we have been given authority over the enemy, that does not mean we can wield that power wherever we like. Jesus always acted under His Father's authority.

> *To move in the power of the Spirit, we must be led by the Spirit.*

Furthermore, we can only bind or loosen that which has already been bound or loosened in heaven. Matthew 16:19 literally says, *whatever you bind on earth will already have been bound in heaven.* We must first be led by the Spirit before we presume to bind or loosen anything. So, as we humbly ask for His guidance and listen, He will faithfully lead us.

Saying *in Jesus' name* at the end of a prayer does not, in and of itself, validate the prayer or give it authority if it is not in line with Jesus' will. When Jesus said: "Whatever you ask in My name, I will do it" (John 14:14), is to pray in accord with His nature and specific desire. As Jesus said: "If you abide in Me, and My words abide in you, ask whatever you wish, and it will be done for you" (John 15:7). As we learn to stay surrendered, dependent and attentive, growing in the knowledge of His ways and listening to what He says, then we can have confidence that we have that for which we have asked (1 John 5:14,15).

Whatever we focus upon will rule our hearts. If we focus on the enemy and what he is doing, then we will find our confidence in Jesus will be undermined. If we focus on the power and love of our resurrected Jesus, who has conquered death itself, we will find our hearts encouraged to stand with Him. The way to overcome the enemy is to focus on the Overcomer, listen to Him, gain His perspective (2 Kings 6:16, 17) and cooperate with what He is doing.

We have not found it necessary to address Satan or demons directly. Why talk with the lying deceiver when we can find out all we need to know from the Holy Spirit of truth? Besides, we have found that speaking directly with demons can be a serious stumbling block to those who have a fascination with the demonic. It also can draw us out from under the covering we have in Christ. The accuser loves to be the center of attention, and we don't want to give him that power.

> *We certainly never ever ridicule the enemy or call him names.*

We have heard some horrific stories of those who have over-stepped their biblical authority and found themselves in serious bondage. If we presume to rise in contempt above the enemy in our own strength, we leave ourselves vulnerable to his schemes. Let us heed this sober warning: "Michael the arch-angel ... did not dare pronounce against him [the devil] a railing judgment but said: 'the Lord rebuke you.' But these men, revile the things which they do not understand ..." (Jude 9, 10).

Effective spiritual warfare is not grounded on binding the enemy but on knowing God is supreme. Declaring the Father's authority, almighty power and victory and worship-ping Him as Lord of all, are used by the Holy Spirit as mighty weapons against the enemy.

Finally, in Chapter 6, we mentioned that once lies have been renounced, they must be replaced by truth that pene-trates our hearts which can be facilitated by declaring and rejoicing in the truth the Father has given in exchange. Jesus makes it clear in Matthew 12:43-45 that we cannot merely remove a spirit and leave empty heart space, or we can be vulnerable to even greater bondage. Once an evil spirit has been removed from our hearts, we must make sure that we have received an exchange from the Lord to replace the heart room vacated by that spirit.

We highly recommend having a trusted and mature believer stand with you as you work through this Renunciation, one who understands the authority we have in Christ and recognizes the strategies of the enemy to undermine the character of God and our true identity in Him.

Renunciation for Spiritual Oppression

Once we have removed the ground we have given to the enemy through renouncing lies, repentance, forgiveness or however God leads, then we can confidently claim our authority in Christ and we may ask:

Father, is there a spirit I have given access to through these lies I have believed?

If yes, *How has this spirit influenced my relationship with You and with others?*

Am I ready to break with this spirit?

If not, you may ask: *What will my life be like if I do break with this spirit?*

Father, I renounce and break off all influence, agreement and authority I have given to the spirit of _____ and I bind that spirit by the authority and power of Jesus and cast it to His feet.

Father, is the spirit of _____ broken off my life now?
If not, you may ask: *What else do I need to do to break with this spirit?*
Am I willing to obey You in this?

I repent for partnering with that spirit and allowing it influence in my life (Be specific).

Father, do You forgive me? (Yes) *Then I receive Your forgiveness and forgive myself.*

Father, what do You have for me in exchange?

If needed, unpack it with Him by asking more questions until it is practical and helpful.

Receive it in your heart by declaring and rejoicing in what He has given.

You may unpack it further by asking: *Father, how can I walk with You so that I can experience the fruit of what You have given?*

CHAPTER 9

Disappointment and Anger toward God

*D*on't skip the next two chapters even if you feel that disappointment and anger toward God or grief and loss are not issues for you.

We are living in a culture in which the spirit of the world (1 Corinthians 2:12) has increasing influence upon all groups of people, whatever their beliefs. We, too, as the church, are not immune to being discipled by our culture. We need to be resolved in our thinking regarding the character of God, His goodness, grace, mercy and redemptive purpose at work in our lives.

Recently, I (Diane) was watching a sci-fi series centering on a worldwide disaster. The hero was about to go out to face the chaos and danger of their situation and said to a girl, *I guess the only thing left is for us to pray.* The girl's response was, *God got us into this mess. I'd rather trust in you.* Almost without exception, the general trend in thinking, being propagated in media and entertainment, is that God is indifferent, impotent or capricious. Our view of God is becoming increasingly shaped by Hollywood and humanism and we have acquired myths about pain and suffering that are not biblical. As the church, we have largely lost any theology of suffering.

Several years ago, an Internet poll asked those over 50 years old to give one word to describe the present generation. Over 70% came back with the same word: *entitled*. We feel we are entitled to an easy life, good health, the right to be married, to have a good job, to become a success if we work hard enough, and if we make the right choices we deserve to be rewarded and recognized. In other words, we should not have to miss out or have things go badly if we perform well and do our best.

Matthew 24:12 says, "... because lawlessness is increased, the love of many will grow cold." With over 60 million displaced people due to wars and hardship, more human trafficking and slavery than ever before in history, the perpetual information overload of disasters and tragedies, and desperate prayers that seem to go unanswered in the face of personal trials, what can we say to those who call into question the goodness of God? We are in a war and our hearts are the battleground.

As believers, what do we do with doubts that rise in our hearts when things just don't seem to make sense? Where do we go in our hearts when we don't get answers to the *why* questions? Too often, we have lost touch with the redemptive purpose of God in our lives, working *within* our circumstances. We have exchanged that redemptive purpose for the demand that for God to be good, He must change our circumstances.

Only by having the eyes of our hearts opened to who God truly is, can we know God intimately. Indeed, the depth of our relationship with Him is rooted in our view of His character. This is why the enemy has worked so hard through the centuries to malign Him, accuse Him and blame Him.

We have found, in meeting one-on-one with hundreds of believers of all ages, that few openly acknowledge anger toward God–especially in "Bible Belt" America. We push it down. We don't admit it. We may seek to maintain the outward appearance of the Christian life. While many may deny actual anger toward God, (after all, what Christian is going to easily admit they are mad at God?), it's often easier for believers to admit they are disappointed in Him. Inevitably then, we lack the inner joy of connection with God Himself and frequently find ourselves frustrated, discouraged, cynical and bitter.

Disappointment with God can simply be because of the parameters He has given us, the things about ourselves we cannot change–our parents and the choices they made, our position in the family, past wounds, our body type, our intelligence, our abilities.

> *If the enemy can destroy our trust in the goodness of God by getting us to partner with him in accusing God, we will distance ourselves from Him and thereby cut ourselves off from the grace and power He offers us to go through the trials and difficulties of life.*

A few years ago, I (Diane) was meeting with a young woman who was a university senior and a mature leader in a large college ministry at our local church. She was spiritually dry and beginning to get in touch with anger and resentment toward God where she found herself not wanting to relate to Him or connect with Him in any way. She was experiencing repressed anger toward God because of having been sexually violated by a neighbor in an ongoing way when she was four and five years old.

The natural question arises in any of our hearts, especially in the face of being victimized: *If God is good, or if God really cared, how could He have let that happen to me?*

73:26). "He only is my rock and my salvation, my stronghold; I shall not be shaken" (Psalm 62:6). Trust placed anywhere else, ultimately, to some degree, brings disappointment.

> *Our faith is not our security and hope. He is.*
> *The object of our faith. Jesus!*

In a fallen and unstable world, we simply cannot experience lasting joy and peace without unshakeable hope. Jesus overcame the temptations, trials and grief of this world, even death itself, and He has made a way for us to join Him in that victory and fill our hearts in the deepest places of need.

When we face disappointing and painful events, what is it that keeps us tender, open and responsive to God?

The Power of Surrender

On January 2, 2015 I (Diane) was diagnosed with Alzheimer's. For 16 weeks I lived with that diagnosis. It was completely out of my control, facing incredible personal loss and loss to my family. Filled with overwhelming emotions, grief and fears I was catapulted into processing these feelings and thoughts with God.

From the beginning He said to me: *Diane, I hold you in my hands as a little baby. I will never let you go.* Experiencing the overwhelming grace of God moment by moment was one of the richest times of sustained fellowship with Him that I have ever experienced. During this time, He gave me a picture of His heart—His arms open wide, leaning toward me with an expression of eagerness on His face, eager to embrace me with grace.

It was as I turned to Him, brought my struggles, fear and pain to Him that He spoke to me, encouraging me, revealing more of His heart to me, and this increased my confidence to

111

come to Him with expectancy. 13 weeks into this diagnosis I was prompted by the Holy Spirit to ask Jesus a question:

What is the love of God made up of?

He said: *The will.*

I asked: *Is it my will fully surrendered to Your will? Is it me saying to You with my whole heart–not my way, but Your way, not my timing but Your timing, not my will but Your will be done?*

He replied: *Your surrender to my will is the triumph of love. It is the point of my most joyous victory, because then I know I have won your heart completely, that you are fully mine. I will take your will and handle it tenderly. With that surrender is a release of power unlike any other. It gives me freedom to move mountains, bless nations and reach into the hearts of others on your behalf. My greatest work is the unseen places where my children surrender their will to me. When my son surrendered His will to me in the Garden of Gethsemane, it did not take the cross out of the way, but it meant resurrection and an empty tomb on the other side.*

When I am willing to surrender my natural life, only then can I experience fully the power of the resurrection and live a supernatural life. I know this is the point at which He healed me. Let me be clear, of course, surrender to His will doesn't guarantee our preferred result, but it does open the door to receive His all-sufficient grace for our hearts, regardless.

Through this trial, I learned so much about the heart of God, and so much about myself; about the power of surrender, linked with faith.

> *Surrender is relational. It is not resignation to my circumstances. It is trust and confidence in the character of God Himself, embracing His will and releasing my preferences.*

This releases Him to fully act on our behalf. At the end of 16 weeks, I went for several hours of final testing at the Memory Research Center in Dallas. The result was average or above in every area for my age. We both were stunned, humbled and, of course, elated.

He is a Redeemer and He will come into every situation, trial or circumstance to redeem it. There is nothing He can't redeem fully. When we get hold of the grace that God offers, it overcomes the weight and oppression of the pain, regret, hopelessness, despair, loss and anger. It is not getting the answers we want but knowing God deeply and personally *in* all our grief.

> *As our hearts are anchored in the heart*
> *of God, we can experience abiding joy*
> *and peace in the face of sorrow.*
> *It is the miracle of God's grace.*

What are the decisions or choices I (Diane) have to make about God and my circumstances to partner with Him in His redemptive purposes in my life? In the midst of disappointment and suffering, here are things I choose to believe:

1. God is for me.
2. God is good, and He is with me in the midst of my circumstances.
3. He feels my pain and His grace is available for me right now.
4. God deeply cares about my struggle and will help me walk intimately with Him in it, so I can receive the grace He offers.

5. God is at work producing for me an "eternal weight of glory" in this "momentary," passing affliction (2 Corinthians 4:17).
6. This struggle does not change the fact that God has good plans for my life.
7. God is an infinite Redeemer, and I will one day see redeeming good come out of this struggle.

In trials, quite naturally, we may want relief, escape, victory, breakthrough, healing, restoration, peace and hope. However, even though these desires may be much more than our own preferences and be from God, they can easily become an idol –coming between us and God. The outcome we want becomes more important to us than our relationship with Him and the way He may want to draw us closer to Himself and gain more in our hearts through this situation.

Although we don't like it, the fact remains that only with trials are we able to find out for ourselves God's amazing ability to comfort us and bring us hope, even if the painful circumstances don't change or don't appear to.

> *The afflicted apostle Paul understood the opportunity that trials afford to know the heart of God:*

"That I may know Him and the power of His resurrection and the fellowship of His sufferings" (Philippians 3:10). Perhaps you have heard the stories of prisoners who find Christ in jail and declare with joy *I am free!* despite knowing they will remain behind bars.

When we see God as He is (1 John 3:2) our questions are answered (John 16:23) and we shall be satisfied (Psalm 17:15). The more we open ourselves to receive from the heart of God, the very source of love, goodness and justice, the more our hearts are fully met, simply because we are made for Him. Offense, indignation, why questions, hesitancy, and unbelief will be exposed and evaporate, and we will fall on our faces in humility and awe as the apostle John did when He saw Jesus in His dazzling beauty. (Revelation 1:17).

Suffering and God's Sovereignty

Overcoming evil through Jesus

When faced with suffering and man's inhumanity to man, the question arises: How can God be both good and powerful? Some argue: *If God is good then, He is not powerful enough to stop it. If He is powerful, then He is not good enough to stop it.* Many conclude that God doesn't care or that He is impotent.

If God overruled evil by brute force it would never solve the problem of evil. If He overruled in one case of evil He would need to do it in every case—and our free will would be gone. Sure, we would be prevented from doing evil, but neither could we choose to love!

God's decision was to enter humanity and suffer with us— and ultimately to overcome evil with love. On the cross, as a man, Jesus felt forsaken by God that He might become the God of those who feel forsaken.

Life is full of contradictions.

> *We may encounter mind-numbing evil. We also encounter breathtaking acts of kindness. Only the cross of Jesus makes sense of this.*

This is why it is the kingpin of the gospel, the good news. Humanism, atheism, Islam, Hinduism, can't do this.

On the throne of the universe is, as Revelation 5:6 literally means, a *freshly slain Lamb*–the one who suffered more than any. This is how He rules. We have no conclusive answer to all the mysteries of suffering, but we do have a gospel that speaks of a God whose heart is in solidarity with all who suffer.

Paul suffered the loss of everything for the sake of knowing Christ. When Nero was torching Christians to light up his garden parties, Peter wrote this: "Beloved, do not be surprised at the fiery ordeal among you, which comes upon you for your testing, as though some strange thing were happening to you" (1 Peter 4:12). Scripture is filled with references to endurance, perseverance, overcoming and victory. Why? Because we are in a war, and *we* are the focus of that war.

The enemy will attempt to destroy our intimacy with God by taking advantage of every circumstance, every trial and every disappointment. God's permissive will can appear indifferent or even cruel. He accuses God so that we distance ourselves from Him and cut ourselves off from His mercy and grace in our circumstances.

Jesus Himself had to learn obedience through suffering. Think of those words He cried out on the cross: "My God, My God, *why* have You forsaken Me?" (Matthew 27:46). As far as we know, at that time He received no answer, yet He still turned to His Father and said, "into Your hands I commit My Spirit" (Luke 23:46).

If we are to stand against the schemes of the devil, because our struggle is not against flesh and blood, our foundation has to be the person and heart of Jesus Christ Himself.

> *The only way we can come to peace about our why questions is to encounter His heart for us.*

As our friend Kurt, a missionary in one of the darkest places on earth, articulated: *Jesus doesn't give us the answer, He becomes the answer.*

If our hope is in outcomes alone or the avoidance of trials, then, as we have said, we will be vulnerable to partnering with the enemy and accusing God, which completely cuts off our access to receiving the grace of God that He promises will meet every need. (Hebrews 4:16; Ephesians 1:7,8). However, as we turn to Him who bore our pain and sorrow (Isaiah 53:4), and listen to His heart for us, we can come to the place where we do not need to insist on answers to the why questions. It does not mean that we do not give voice to our pain, anger and confusion, or even cry out in anguish as Jesus did from the cross, *My God, My God, why?* In hearing His heart, we too can move past the *why* to say with Jesus, *into Your hands I commit my spirit.*

We must ask ourselves and help others to ask the *what* and *how* questions.

What are You doing in this Lord? What do You want to accomplish in me?

How do You want me to cooperate with You? How can I bring glory to You in this situation?

Unless we are tending our hearts with the negative thoughts and emotions that surface during a trial, we will not be able to overcome. Any disappointment that is not acknowledged will not go away, so we must bring it to Jesus and let Him meet us there.

Recognizing and renouncing anger and disappointment with God

How do we recognize anger and disappointment toward God? We tend to push it down. We often don't admit it. We distance ourselves from God. We may stay busy, even doing things we think are for God, to avoid facing our disappointment or anger toward Him.

Some possible indications of anger or disappointment toward God

1. Outbursts of anger.
2. We cannot hear God. We cannot receive what He says.
3. Long periods of spiritual dryness.
4. Walls or barriers we have erected against God or others
5. Difficulty trusting God because of lies that arise in our thinking:
    He doesn't care. My pain doesn't really matter to Him. He doesn't understand my pain. He doesn't have good things for me. He withholds from me what I really need.
6. Patterns of negative expectation. Self-pity. Being a victim.
7. Comparison. When we compare ourselves with others, we are saying that what God is attempting to do in our lives, conforming us more into the likeness of His Son, isn't fair.

> *If we are harboring anger and disappointment with God, we are far more deeply wounded by choosing to partner with the enemy to accuse Him, than any other kind of wound we could ever receive from someone else!*

Jesus says in Luke 7:23: "Blessed is he who does not take offense at Me."

If grief or loss is a hindrance to you releasing disappointment and anger toward God, we recommend going to Chapter 10, *Processing Grief and Loss,* and then returning to this chapter.

JOURNALING DISAPPOINTMENT AND ANGER TOWARD GOD

Turn your heart and mind to Him.
Quiet the noise.
Invite Him to sit right there with you as you listen.
Worship and give Him thanks.
Do not rush. Take time over each question.
(Ecclesiastes 5:1,2: "Draw near to listen ... do not be hasty ... or [lit. hurry your heart].")

As you work through the following questions, ask the Father if you should go onto the next question or stay where you are and process with Him more deeply.

Father, what are the areas in my life where I have been disappointed?

(family, circumstances, abilities, appearance, etc.) List them.

Have I held any of these things against You in my heart?

When I compare myself with others, what am I believing about You?

Father, have I partnered with the spirit of entitlement?

How do You want me to respond to this?

Father, what unsurrendered rights am I holding onto?

Father, why am I holding onto them?

What do You have to say to me that will help me surrender them?

***If there is any disappointment or anger toward God, work through the following Renunciation.

Renunciation: Anger and Disappointment Toward God

Father, am I willing to fully release my anger and disappointment toward You?

If not, *Father, what will my life be like if I hold onto my anger toward You?*

How will my life change if I release my anger toward You?

Father, what do You have to say to me about my inability to come to complete peace with You for allowing _____ to take place?

Holy Spirit, will You help me to release all my anger toward Father God?

Father, what is the lie I have believed about You?
  Father, I renounce the lie that You ...

I must recognize my agreement with the enemy to accuse God.

Father, I repent for hardening my heart and partnering with the enemy to accuse and blame You.
  I repent for grieving You by not believing in Your love for me.
  Father, do You forgive me? (Yes) Then I forgive myself.

I must recognize the deception and power of this spirit.

Father, I renounce and sever all influence, agreement, partnership and authority I have given to the enemy in joining with him to accuse You and I break off this lying and deceiving spirit by the authority and power of Jesus and cast it to His feet.

Father, what do You have for me in exchange for anger and disappointment toward You?

Father, have I come to complete peace with You?

GOING DEEPER:
God's View vs. Man's View of Suffering

All people, Christians and non-Christians, will suffer. Nobody is immune. However, Christians, by the power of the indwelling Holy Spirit, are able to experience His comfort and even joy in those trials. This is the stunning hope we offer unbelievers. Not a pain-free life, but a life in Christ where we are able to experience His love and peace no matter what. The more we receive the authentic comfort Jesus offers, the more we can comfort others. "The Father of mercies and God of all comfort who comforts us in all our affliction so that we may be able to comfort those who are in any affliction with the comfort with which we ourselves are comforted by God" (2 Corinthians 1:3, 4).

Myths About Suffering

Myth: When we are living in God's will, living godly lives, we should experience few hardships.

Truth: We must go through many hardships to enter the kingdom of God; we were destined for trials (Acts 14:22; 1 Thessalonians 3:3).

Myth: Suffering means something is wrong. It is an abnormal state.

Truth: Suffering is normal and inevitable in the Christian life (2 Timothy 3:12).

Myth: Suffering has no redeeming or positive results.

Truth: God uses suffering for our good, to conform us to the likeness of His son (Romans 8:28-29).

Myth: Suffering means we can have no joy. It robs us of the choice to rejoice.

Truth: We are free to rejoice in our suffering. "... though tested by fire ... you greatly rejoice with joy inexpressible" (1 Peter 1:7,8).

Myth: Spiritual people don't hurt emotionally when they suffer.

Truth: Spiritual people feel many painful emotions when they suffer (Mark 14:33-34; 2 Corinthians 2:4).

Myth: If God really loves us, He won't let us suffer very much. His love means that He will put a hedge around us to keep us from terrible trials.

Truth: He didn't prevent His own son from suffering. He didn't prevent Paul, Peter, John the Baptist and others He loved from suffering greatly.

Myth: As Christians, we should not suffer in this life.

Truth: In fact, we are called to suffer for Jesus (Philippians 1:29; 1 Peter 2:20-21).

Myth: When bad things happen, God merely allows them.

Truth: "But He [Jesus] was delivered up to you by the predetermined plan of God" (Acts 2:22-23). His redemptive plan and purpose is far greater than we can see.

If there are any truths mentioned above that you have difficulty receiving, use it as an opportunity to ask Jesus what insight He has to help you.

JOURNAL - God's View vs. Myths of Suffering

Father, do I believe any of these myths about suffering and hardship?

Father, tell me why I have been inclined to believe this?

Father, what has been the impact on my life and my attitudes due to these lies?

Renounce the specific lies. Repent.

Father, what is the truth I need to know? What insight do You have for me here?

How do You want me to guard against the infiltration of lies about suffering and remain free to walk in the truth?

Father, do I need to repent for any anger or disappointment toward You?

If necessary, repent thoroughly.

Father, have I come to complete peace with You?
If not, pursue this with Him further. Do not let it remain!

CHAPTER 10

Processing Grief and Loss

"It was a long time before I came to the realization that it is in our acceptance of what is given (our circumstances) that God gives Himself ... This grief, this sorrow, this total loss that empties my hands and breaks my heart, I may if I will, accept, and by accepting it, I find in my hands something to offer. And so, I give it back to Him, who in mysterious exchange He gives Himself to me."

Elizabeth Elliot – *These Strange Ashes*

He is called "the God of *all* comfort" (2 Corinthians 1:3; emphasis added). There is no loss so distant nor so great that He cannot meet us there with life, peace, hope and yes, even joy.

In 2006, we were returning from town where a family who had lost their baby on the delivery table had a memorial celebration of their child's life. Rick turned to me in the car and made the sincere comment, that he was sorry he had been oblivious when our first baby died in a miscarriage some 26 years earlier and that he didn't lead us to seek God to give that child a name. Even though that loss had been so long ago, and even though I had since had the joy of raising a beautiful daughter, I totally lost it, shocked and surprised at the sorrow and grief that rose to the surface.

We felt we should ask God's forgiveness for not inviting Him into that place in the past and were led to intentionally set aside time to grieve that loss and seek the Lord for a name for that child. It was not something that occurred quickly, and Rick was not glib about hearing from God in this situation. So, it was not until some weeks later that he called me into his study and I found him sitting on the floor with his Bible open and tears on his face. He had been led by the Holy Spirit to the book of the prophet Samuel and shared the insight he had been given.

We know more about the early childhood of Samuel than any other person in Scripture. Three different times it says of Samuel that he ministered to the Lord. He rested in the temple of the Lord where the ark of God was (1 Samuel 3:3) and responded to the voice he heard calling him. Rick shared that he felt the Lord said to him, *You have a son and his name is Samuel.*

Rick understood the Lord was revealing that our son had not been called to death but to life, and that his life was with God and perhaps that Samuel was ministering to the Lord. The power of the Holy Spirit was so real in that moment. We rejoiced that we had a son who we would meet one day, and we knew he was with the Lord. As Rick said, *What more could I hope for, in the life of a son? Would I rather he was here so we could enjoy the Lord together while we're windsurfing?* In all the years since, we have not lost that sense that we have a son, our daughter has a brother and that our family is complete—all that God intended.

> *It was through that experience that I received the revelation that no loss is so distant that God is not able and motivated to redeem that loss and meet us with comfort and even joy.*

Grief and loss can touch very deep places that take time to process and have many layers.

It was in being met by God in the way we were regarding Samuel that I was reminded of an earlier part of the process many years before. We were living in Tasmania, and I was a part of a group of women who met to support and pray for one another on a regular basis.

It was April, eight years after the miscarriage, and as we were sharing together, I realized my need was to come out from under a sense of heaviness and sadness. I realized that a pattern of undefined heaviness and sadness happened to me every year around that same time. This struck me because although I have suffered great losses, depression or ongoing anxiety were not a part of my experience.

As the group prayed about this heaviness, the Lord showed me that it was eight years earlier I miscarried the baby who would become known to us, 18 years later, as our son Samuel. So, it was years after the loss before I was able to face it with the Lord, cast off that repeating pattern of sadness, begin to experience release and comfort, and move toward healing and wholeness.

How can we grieve with God and find relief? First, it makes all the difference to know that Jesus perfectly understands our need to grieve and is eager to meet us and help us as we do. He, more than any of us, understood the need to cry out and grieve freely with His Father. "In the days of His earthly life, Jesus offered up both [specific] petitions and [urgent] supplications [for that which He needed] with fervent crying and tears to the One who was [always] able to save Him from death …" (Hebrews 5:7 AMP).

It is the act of intentionally choosing to process, or more accurately, *grieve with God,* that opens the way to surrender to Him our pain and sorrow, let Him lift it off us and carry it for us. As it says in Isaiah 53:3 and 4 (AMP): "A Man of sorrows and pain and acquainted with grief … But He has borne our griefs, and He has carried our sorrows and pains."

We don't pretend to have expertise in this area, but we have seen many with deeply painful circumstances and wounding find peace with God and themselves as they discover His amazing ability to embrace us with grace and bring comfort and healing in the very midst of their suffering.

So, how can we grieve with God and find relief? It is very helpful, if not essential for us for us to distinguish the difference between lie-based pain and truth-based pain if we are to effectively meet with God in our losses and receive all He has for us. Most of us have encountered a combination of both.

Lie-based Pain and Truth-based Pain

Lie-based pain is when, in the midst of any loss or trial, we agree with the enemy's accusations of God and ourselves so we experience the pain of believing that God does not care. He's abandoned me. He's removed His protection. He's punishing me. My pain does not matter to Him. I'm worthless. There's something wrong with me.

Lie-based pain requires us to renounce the lie, repent for partnering with the enemy and then receive the personal, rhema word from God in exchange for the lie.

Truth-based pain is when there is valid loss suffered, but not as the result of any lies we believed. This can be pain

we experience due to wounds caused by the sins of
Or perhaps we have sacrificed in obedience to God a
has resulted in great loss or emotional pain. Maybe ... .
result of a traumatic event, such as a miscarriage or loss of
a loved one.

If we have been wounded by others, we need to forgive
them. However, that can be a real struggle. Sometimes,
before we can fully forgive, we may have to release our grief
and loss to God. We may need to grieve the loss that was
caused by the wound. Perhaps it was the loss of innocence
or the loss of childhood that was taken from us. Maybe it is
the loss of not having the mother or father we needed. As
we bring God our pain, share our raw feelings with Him and
lay our pain before Him, we often find we are able to forgive
and receive His comfort and strength.

Even though we may have truly forgiven someone for
wounding us, we may still carry the sadness of those losses
as a result of those wounds—truth-based pain. This is where
we need to give our pain to Jesus and trust Him to lift it off us.

So, we forgive for the wounds we have received from
others, but we never forgive God because He has never done
anything wrong. If necessary, we must repent for accusing
God and renounce the lies and accusations against Him.

When Truth-based and Lie-based Pain are Entangled

A situation with a mother of a five-month-old, lost because
of SIDS, very clearly illustrates this combined and often debilitating process of being entangled in the lie-based pain that
immobilized and led to despair, as well as the valid losses
and resulting grief of the truth-based pain.

She and her husband had rejoiced daily in the wonder of
having their first child and she thrived and rejoiced in her role as

129

a new mother. When I met with this young, yet mature Christian woman following the death of her daughter, both she and her husband were serving God's purpose through cutting-edge technology that had the potential to transform third-world communities. Understandably, due to her severe loss, she was still essentially immobilized in being able to move forward to healing and acceptance and to find real comfort or hope.

When we asked God in Listening Prayer* what the lies were that she had begun to believe as the result of her loss, this is what she felt she heard. *That God is impotent. My pain doesn't matter to Him. He is punishing me. I am a bad mom. God did not value my daughter's life.* It was in the actual naming of the lies that she was able to get enough insight to recognize that by faith she had to renounce partnering with the enemy and these lies about God and herself.

This opened the door for her to begin to bring to God the valid losses, the truth-based pain, of never seeing her daughter grow up, marry and have children of her own and for the missed opportunities of joy and fulfillment in knowing this child and the loss that would always be a part of their lives.

-----

* Footnote:

Listening Prayer is now a term used by a variety of ministries, often with different meanings. The ministry that the Lord has developed through us, after having received widely from the body of Christ, is simply where we facilitate a person in a sustained conversation with God, so they might encounter Him and, if needed, overcome hindrances to intimacy. Our goal is to equip the person to draw directly from God as their primary source.

Within weeks, as I met with her again, she had the joy of sharing that God had revealed to her that her daughter had given her a legacy and her life here on earth had mattered. A large part of that legacy was the growth in intimacy in her own relationship with God and being able to bring hope and comfort to others who have experienced similar losses. Both she and her husband are actively and intentionally reaching out to other parents who have lost a child to SIDS. Each year their family and friends release balloons to celebrate her daughter's life and the legacy they have been given by her.

Painful losses like this may be grieved in layers as they surface throughout our lifetime but knowing the Father's eagerness to embrace us and encourage us, brings fresh opportunities for sweet encounters and gratitude.

Guarding Our Hearts

We cannot avoid disappointment and discouragement, but our response to it is critical. As we have noted, if we hold onto our pain, the enemy will use it to accuse God and keep us suffering because of it. We may shut our hearts down and harden them toward God or spiral down toward depression. Grief that is not processed with God will remain in our hearts and it will be added to by other disappointments, building in layers so that subsequent loss will trigger previous loss. However, each time we take our grief to God, grieve it with Him and process it with Him, He will prove again and again to be "the God of *all* comfort."

Most of us realize that pain may surface in layers over time, and so, as it does, we can give each layer of grief or loss to Him, ask Him what He has for our hearts in that moment and receive His grace and comfort. Then, as subsequent layers arise, we find ourselves able to move over in our hearts more quickly until that sorrow or loss becomes a place of bittersweet intimacy with God.

I would never have been able to experience the peace or even the joy I did during my experience with Alzheimer's and the ongoing comfort of God for all the layers of loss and grief if I had not processed my emotion and sorrow and sought to bring every fearful or negative thought captive as they came up in that 16-week journey.

As we mentioned, our loss may be the loss of our childhood, the loss of innocence or the loss of having a dysfunctional family where we were not protected and cared for. We must come to the place of recognizing this was not love. We were not loved. This can be excruciatingly painful! Yet God wants to comfort us in these deep places.

We grieve loss by pouring out our hearts to God in total honesty, telling Him exactly how we feel. God is not shockable because, of course, He knows it all anyway. We may cry out and say: *This stinks! I hate this!* This is biblical. Check out David's cry while in a cave hiding from King Saul who hunted him.

> "I cry aloud with my voice to the Lord …
> I pour out my complaint before Him;
> I declare my trouble before Him,
> When my spirit was overwhelmed within me,
> You knew my path,
> In the way where I walk
> They have hidden a trap for me …
> For there is no one who regards me;
> There is no escape for me;
> No one cares for my soul,
> I cried out to the Lord;
> I said, 'You are my refuge,
> Give heed to my cry,

For I am brought very low ..."' (Psalm 142:1-6).

"In order to abide in Christ and enjoy God's presence, we must learn not to pretend to be okay. Withholding our true feelings blocks the development of an intimate relationship with God" says Jan Johnson in *Enjoying the Presence of God* (p.59).

We have a Father who is the only one who knows exactly what we need, and He longs to meet our hearts. This is what Jesus died for.

We may ask the Father: "What do I need to grieve?" Journal what He tells you then go to Him with each thing He has highlighted until you are able to release your pain to Him and receive all He has for your heart in exchange.

Someone once said, "The cross is where pain and trauma meet resurrection." The reality is that deep grief and abiding joy can co-exist, and this is the miracle of God's grace and the mystery of the God of all comfort.

> *There are depths of intimacy with God and an understanding of His love for us that can only be experienced in our suffering.*
> *(Jan Johnson)*

JOURNAL PROCESSING GRIEF AND LOSS WITH GOD

Lie-based pain – God does not care, God has abandoned me, I'm worthless, there's something wrong with me. Lie-based pain requires us to renounce the lie and repent for partnering with the enemy.

Truth-based pain – Lingering sadness, loss of childhood or innocence, I was not loved, this was not love, loss of relationship I always wanted with Dad or the kind of Mom I needed, inability to conceive, great loss in the face of sacrifice or difficult circumstances.

When great pain or intolerable loss has occurred, we may need to forgive but we must grieve the loss in the presence of God and yield the burden of our pain and sorrow to Him so that we are able to receive His comfort.

To grieve our pain and loss with God and to pour out our hearts before Him may need to be repeated as layers of pain surface.

Grieving apart from God gives the enemy access to accuse God because of our pain. Or, we can try to avoid the pain. If we ignore our pain and don't give God the opportunity to meet us in it, it does not go away!

ASK HIM: *Jesus, what do I need to grieve?*
Write down whatever He tells you.
Take each one and truthfully tell Him how you feel. God is not shock-able!

Offer all grief and sadness to Him to lift off you and carry for you upon His own body.

"Surely, our grief and pain He Himself bore, and our sorrows He carried" (Isaiah 53:4). If it is helpful, ask Him to show you Himself on the cross and you lifting it up to Him.

Jesus, I yield my pain up to You and let You bear it for me. I thank You that You feel my pain and that You desire to be the "God of all comfort" for me.

Jesus, what do You give my heart in the place of my pain?

Receive His exchange with thankfulness and worship.

CHAPTER 11

False Identities

*I*f we have become accustomed to a lie and have allowed it to determine something about our identity or value, we can end up taking on the message of that lie as a false identity. *I am an orphan (abandoned). I am worthless. I am fearful.* This false identity is a demonic attachment that becomes so familiar that, for the sake of simplicity, we call a familiar spirit.* These familiar spirits and how to overcome them will now be addressed in this chapter.

As we have stated, the lies of the enemy are targeted to kill intimacy with God by undermining our trust in God or our true identity in Christ. As the apostle John states clearly: "We know that we are of God, and the whole world lies in the power of the evil one. And we know that the Son of God has come, and has given us understanding, in order that we might *know Him* who is true [the true character of the Father], and *we are in Him* who is true, in His Son Jesus Christ [our true identity]" (1 John 5:19, 20; emphasis added).

Footnote:
This is not to be confused with familial spirits, spiritual strongholds which may be passed down through family lines and which may also be false identities.

135

In this chapter, we will focus on how the enemy has undermined our identity in Christ with devastating effect and how we can reclaim our true identity and walk free to enjoy whom the Father has created us to be.

The power of who we believe we are

Say, for example, as a believer I am tempted to lust and the Holy Spirit faithfully warns me not to give in to it. If I choose to give in to lust, I am rejecting the covering of the blood of Jesus and opening myself to the enemy. By doing so, I am vulnerable to giving access to a demonic spirit of lust that will need to be broken off in Jesus' name.

However, if I continue to reject the checks of the Holy Spirit and choose to partner with the spirit of lust, I can easily become attached to that spirit in a stronger way. As a believer, I may hate the fact that I am in the habit of giving in to lust or I may feel guilty and ashamed about it, but I am also getting something from lust that I enjoy, even if only momentarily. Now, instead of simply having given access to a spirit of lust, I have become so bonded to it that I see myself as a lustful person. I am convinced that I am inherently lustful. It's who I am. It's my natural propensity. It's in my DNA. This is an insidious lie!

Once I am deceived into believing this, then it's simple for the accuser to convince me that I'm stuck and will never truly be free. It's easier to fight something that is attacking me from without, but how can I fight something that is part of me? Now that I consider myself essentially lustful and weak in resisting those kinds of temptations, how easy it is for the enemy to tempt me with lust. I'm already half way over the fence, and it doesn't take much for the enemy to pull me down into further bondage and addictive flesh patterns.

Too often I (Rick) hear Christians say, *I'm a sinner saved by grace.* The reasoning is that if we continue to sin, it must be patently obvious that we are still sinners. This is simply not true, and in fact, it actually sets us up for failure. A sinner's natural propensity is to sin. We didn't have to learn how to sin. We were born that way. No wonder so many believers feel that despite their efforts, they are in a hopeless battle against sin.

You may well have heard about some ill-treated and emaciated prisoners of war who were set free but who wanted to stay, confounding the liberating troops. They had been so subjugated and broken and had become so used to being prisoners that they felt uncomfortable with freedom and leaving their confinement. They were stuck in their old identity.

Many believers still gravitate to Jeremiah 17:9: "The heart is more deceitful than all else and is desperately sick." Consequently,

> *they feel trapped and have been duped into anticipating an ongoing and discouraging struggle against sinful flesh patterns.*

This thinking ignores the finished work of Christ to crucify our sinful nature. God makes it clear through the prophet Ezekiel (11:19, 20): "I ... shall put a new spirit within them. And I shall take the heart of stone out of their flesh and give them a heart of flesh, that they may walk in My statutes ..."

Romans 5:19 states simply the revolutionary transaction that Christ accomplished for us through His death and resurrection: "For as through one man's disobedience the many were made sinners, even so through the obedience of the One the many will be made righteous."

It couldn't be clearer: "While we *were* still sinners, Christ died for us" (Romans 5:8; emphasis added). As believers we are no longer sinners! What a Savior!

As we receive Jesus' finished work on the cross on our behalf and His Spirit takes up residence in us, we are born again. We are a new species! "... our old self was crucified with Him, that our body of sin might be done away with ['made powerless'] that we should no longer be slaves to sin" (Romans 6:6).

In my experience, very few believers are convinced of the truth that, not only were our sins nailed to the cross, *we* were! What Jesus accomplished was more than make the way for us to be clean and forgiven. He dealt with the source of our problem, "the sin-producing factory." (Watchman Nee – *The Normal Christian Life*, p.43). The power of our sinful nature was broken by Jesus' death on our behalf! We have been born again with a new heart that loves God and hates sin. We are now indwelled by the Holy Spirit and are one spirit with Him (1 Corinthians 6:17). This is the power of the Spirit of Jesus who lived a sinless life, and who now lives within us!

Let us not write off the following declaration by the apostle Paul as if it could not possibly be true of the likes of us—because it is. "I have been crucified with Christ; and it is no longer I who live, but *Christ lives in me*" (Galatians 2:20; emphasis added)

Of course, we have old, bad habits, old tracks in our thinking, old desires that we may gravitate towards or which the enemy brings to mind convincing us that, deep down, nothing has changed, and we are still the same old person we have always been. However, our thoughts, feelings and will are in the process of being transformed and renewed as we choose to submit to the authority of the Holy Spirit in our spirit. Those negative and sinful impulses do not spring from the new nature we have in Christ. Moreover, do you realize that not all your thoughts originate from yourself? Remember that we have an enemy who is on the attack.

Paul goes on to say: "We too all formerly lived in the lusts of our flesh, indulging the desires of the flesh and the mind, and *were by nature* children of wrath" (Ephesians 2:3; emphasis added). This means that the desires of our flesh are no longer sourced in our true nature!

"… lay aside the old self … with the deceitful lusts … be renewed in the spirit of your mind and put on *the new self, which in the likeness of God has been created in righteousness and holiness* of the truth" (Ephesians 4:22-24; emphasis added). Wow!

> *Our new self is inherently righteous and holy–like our true Father.*

That's why we are called saints or holy ones.

To look in the mirror and call yourself a saint may be to you a real stretch. When we feel, based on our behavior, that it's more genuine to identify as a sinner, despite what the scripture clearly says, we begin to see the devastating deception of the accuser.

Romans 6:11 goes further: "Even so consider yourselves to be dead to sin, but alive to God in Christ Jesus." In Christ, we have been recreated inherently righteous. Our natural propensity is to honor God. We are, according to our new nature, wholeheartedly and fully responsive to God. To sin is repulsive to our true identity. Who we are now, by nature, hates it!

Our problem is that if we buy the enemy's lies, believe we are stuck with our old nature and that we can never fundamentally change or that we are going to have to live with our bondages, then

> *we actually consider ourselves to be alive to sin and be dead, or at least slow to respond, to God!*

No wonder the accuser focuses so relentlessly on undermining our true identity in Christ to nullify the victory He has won for us and cripple the church.

Of course, no matter how mature we are in Christ, we will always have to make choices to resist temptation and respond to God. It is so much easier, however, to overcome old flesh patterns and cooperate with the Holy Spirit once we know in our hearts that sin no longer has any appeal to the new person Christ has made us to be.

> *Who we truly believe ourselves to be will determine how we act!*

That's why it is so critical for us to receive our true identity as believers from God Himself, the only one who really knows us.

"Therefore, do not let sin reign in your mortal body that you should obey its lusts ... but present yourselves to God as those *alive from the dead*, and your members as instruments of righteousness to God" (Romans 6:12, 13; emphasis added).

Far too often we dwell upon our failure and the enemy's inroads–and that's right where he wants us. It's high time we contemplate the stunning transformation. of who Jesus has made us to be. Let's take to heart, appreciate and enjoy the immensely greater power of the resurrection life of the Holy Spirit now resident in us as believers!

A familiar spirit

As I have prayed with hundreds of people in recent years, I have yet to find any Jesus follower, no matter how mature, who has not embraced a false identity, and usually there are at least several. In my experience, people have actually identified with most of their demonic strongholds. They have assumed this is who they are. What havoc the enemy has created in the church as a result!

As we discussed in Chapter 3, when we believe the lies of the enemy, we partner with him, so we will need to renounce the lie and may also need to break off demonic spirits that we have given access to–the power behind the lie.

For simplicity's sake, as we mentioned earlier, we call false identities *familiar spirits* because we have become accustomed to them and have bonded with them, even if our new nature hates them. As with all the enemy's enticements, we may feel we are gaining something, even if momentarily, and so we may be reluctant to give up this false view of ourselves. We may prefer it because we are comfortable with it. We may even justify it because we are convinced we need it to be safe, recognized or validated.

Furthermore, because these strongholds are so familiar to us and we are so used to them, we may have difficulty recognizing them and the open door we are giving to the enemy. And, of course, the deceiver will do all he can to keep us in the dark, so we are unable to deal with them. Here again, it is critical for us to ask the Father to reveal any false identity we are walking in. I love the way the Holy Spirit scatters the darkness with His blazing light, exposes the enemy's tactics and gives us clarity so we can partner with Him and walk free.

Some common false identities include an orphan spirit, or spirits of self-hatred, fear of rejection, performance, self-reliance, control and lust. It's easy to understand how some of these strongholds may be linked and even feed off each other.

Perhaps I felt abandoned (orphan)
which led me to believe I was worthless (self-hatred),
which opened the door to the fear of rejection,
which led me to believe I needed to perform for approval,
or that I needed to take care of myself (self-reliance, control)
and so, I seek validation and comfort in lust.

When we walk in a familiar spirit, we see life through this filter or lens, and it can have far-reaching, destructive consequences.

> *Every bondage to the enemy
> brings with it blinding deception.*

We may practice ungodly flesh patterns to protect and defend the stronghold that we have identified with because we are deceived into thinking it has some benefit. For example, if I believe I am a lustful person I may also practice lying, decep-tion, hiddenness and defensiveness. I may, in fact, deny the devastating impact that lust is having on myself and others.

If I have identified with self-reliance, for instance, I may be convinced I have no choice but to live this way. I feel pressure to take care of myself and solve my own problems, unable to fully rest in the assurance that God can be trusted to help me.

One of my strongholds

Some years ago, the Father revealed to me (Rick) that I had lived most of my life with a stronghold of negative expectation. I grew up in Australia which, in my experience, can tend to have a view of life that the glass is half empty. I figured that it made sense to not expect too much, to be braced for setbacks, because this would protect me from disappointment. I thought I was wise and simply being realistic.

It was a deep, underlying lack of joy that seemed to permeate my life that prompted me to ask the Father about it. He told me that negative expectation had become like a pet rabbit that I held to my neck and stroked. It was comfortable and familiar. I had identified with it. It felt like it was just the way I had always been, as though it was part of my normal self as a believer. But, He said,

> *this thing you are petting is a viper and it's sucking the life out of you!*

Startled, it was as though I awoke from a seductive dream, my eyes opened to the reality of my deception. I needed that bucket of cold water in my face to bring me to my senses! I repented and broke with the false identity of negative expectation. It had not only had robbed me of joy, but it hindered me from anticipating the Father's grace and made me reluctant to walk through doors He opened for me. Far too frequently, I expected that behind those doors awaited more sacrifice, loss and hardship. I had become gun shy. I wasn't looking forward to the future.

Furthermore, although I had never recognized it or faced it, the Father showed me that, deep down, I had felt like He had gone out of His way to make life hard for me. I felt that I had done more than my fair share of time on the backside of the desert, being humbled. I made sense of those decades by figuring that He was refining me, purging my heart and increasing my dependence on Him, although

I often wondered if I was just wandering in circles. Now I admitted that, in my heart, I resented the fact that I felt like it had gone on far too long. Never in my life had I acknowledged that I was disappointed in God. I had always been grateful to Him for His immense kindness to me. But I knew it was true. It broke me.

The Father again gently revealed that beneath my negative expectation was, in His words, an evil heart of unbelief. I had come into agreement with the enemy and bought the lie that God was unfair. They were strong, hard words for me to hear. I understood that if I didn't hate this place I had moved to in my heart, I would continue to play with it and never deal with it in the ruthless way it required if I was to be free.

I repented for agreeing with the enemy's accusation and questioning the Father's kindness. I renounced the lie and broke with that familiar spirit of negative expectation in Jesus' name. This was the beginning of a dramatic shift in my whole view of life. It was huge!

In exchange for negative expectation He gave me a new identity of joyful anticipation. Of course, as challenges arise, I need to choose to put on my new identity and live in the reality of who He has created me to be. But, it has been so much easier to move over once the stronghold had been broken.

In exchange for unbelief in the heart of the Father, He has given me a fresh capacity to anticipate His kindness and look forward to the future, no matter what it looks like or feels like. He always trades up! He is so incredibly good!

When a godly attribute becomes twisted

One of the reasons some of the false identities we embrace go undetected, is because they appear to be worthy attributes on the surface. For example, many are quick to

own that they are performers, even driven, becaus
feel they accomplish much, even for God, and are ther
unlike those who are passive, lacking motivation and
accept the status quo.

> *For this reason, this stronghold is frequently validated in the church!*

The problem is that those who are driven usually find they cannot shut down their inner motor and truly rest. Cloaked in godly zeal, they may not recognize they have become slaves. Of course, Jesus never drives us with a whip. As a good shepherd, He leads us and calls us to follow. True to our new nature, we are responders not performers.

A few years ago, the Father showed me I had embraced a false identity of obligation. It manifested like this. When I was asked to address a need, frequently an inner urge would rise up where I felt compelled to address it. This seemed to me to be a noble attribute. After all, aren't we supposed to lay our lives down for others and be a servant of all? The problem was that the needs of others would usually take priority over those in my own family. I justified this by reasoning that, relatively speaking, my family was doing fine, and these others were in greater need. As a result, my family often only received the leftovers.

But, there was a bigger problem. Focused time with God Himself was being squeezed out of my life. Far too often, I was more highly motivated to respond to the needs of others and so I relegated Him to fit in with my other priorities. I would justify it with the thought that God is always around, and I could catch up with Him later. And besides I am serving Him when I serve others, aren't I?

If I had asked Him before responding to these needs and been prepared to follow His direction, it would have been an entirely different matter. But, asking Him while holding onto my preference, my idol, was asking with my fingers in my ears. As Samuel said: "Has the Lord as much delight in ... sacrifices as in obeying the voice of the Lord?" (1 Samuel 15:22).

Underneath this spirit of obligation lurked pride that others were looking to me for help and the desire to be well thought of. More than this, I lacked confidence in Jesus to take care of those in need that I should say no to, believing myself indispensable.

> *Logically, I would never agree with these thoughts, but my anxious behavior and lack of joy revealed the truth I held in my heart.*

Around the same time, Diane, after a conversation with the Father, recognized she had been walking under a familiar spirit of false responsibility, similar to obligation.

One of the pressures that I had come under was a growing desire from church leaders for Diane and me to train what we call Listening Prayer Ministry facilitators to help people in two-way conversation with God, to process heart issues that hinder enjoyable intimacy with Him. While I knew that this ministry had developed and grown due to the Lord's initiative and grace, I found myself losing my joy as I came under the weight and chafing yoke of the lie that I was obligated, that I was responsible to make things happen, even though that was never the heart of my church leaders.

As I asked the Father about it, He told me to write in my Listening Journal in capitals, THIS IS MY WORK. Then He told me to underline MY. He told me that this ministry was His idea, that He had begun it and He would finish it.

> *He explained that my only responsibility*
> *the face of the demands was to do what*
> *asked me to do and leave the rest to Him.*
> *The buck stopped with Him.*

He would carry the heavy side of the yoke. After all, Jesus did say that the yoke He has for us is pleasant (Matthew 11:30). He reminds me every now and then that if I am coming under pressure and strain from a problem or heavy load, then I have clearly picked up a burden that He wants to carry.

After I repented of my skewed motives of pride and seeing myself as indispensable, I broke off this familiar spirit of obligation in Jesus' name and immediately felt a huge weight lift off and a freedom from heaviness that was amazing to me, in spite of the fact that outward pressures actually increased. When a problem arose, I would thank Jesus that the problem was His. I didn't know what He would do about it but told Him to let me know if He wanted me to help in any way, otherwise I would not take it on. This was simply revolutionary in learning to be a carefree yet responsible child, confident that Jesus will take good care of what was stealing my joy, so I could rest in Him.

What follows is a simple tool that can be used to identify and break off any false identity. It's important that when we break off a spirit, we understand how that spirit has affected our behavior. We may ask the Father to show us how this false identity has affected our relationship with Him and with others. He will show us the ways in which the enemy has deceived us and robbed us. After He has set us free, we will be able to anticipate His grace as we walk in our new identity in those kinds of situations. As we ask Him, He will give us fresh perspective and renewed confidence in our true identity and His love for us.

Renunciation of False identities or Familiar Spirits

A false identity is based on a lie about who we really are. We may hate it but feel stuck and we accept it. We identify with a demonic spirit such as orphan, self-condemnation, worthlessness, fear of rejection, performance, self-reliance, control, lust, rebellion, victim, etc. We may think we must be this way to be accepted or receive comfort. A false identity feels familiar and safe. But, we give the enemy access to keep us in bondage.

In Christ we are created righteous (Ephesians 4:24). Who we truly are is dead to sin and alive to God (Romans 6:11). We may be fearful of giving up a false identity and unsure of how to be or act without it. We may feel vulnerable. This place of dependency is our opportunity to hear from God who we are and how we can partner with Him to live out our true identity.

DISCOVER:
Father, have I been walking in a false identity?

What is the familiar spirit that I have been accommodating?

If self-hatred is identified, go to the Self-Hatred Renunciation.

If there are several, ask: *What is the familiar spirit I have identified with the most strongly?*

148

You may ask: *Father, what has been the impact on my rela-tionship with You/others by joining with this spirit?*

You may ask*: Is there anyone I need to forgive for partnering with this familiar spirit?*

Father, am I willing to break with this familiar spirit?
> *If fearful or uncertain of breaking with the spirit,*
> *you may ask: Father, what will my life be like*
> *if I don't break with this spirit?*
> *If I do break ....?*

Perhaps: *If I give up this familiar spirit, what would You give me in exchange?*

RENOUNCE: *By the authority and power of Jesus, I renounce and break off all influence, partnership and authority I have given to the familiar spirit of _____ and I break off all unholy soul ties and any false identity from that spirit.*

(Suggested for strongest, optional for others)
In the name of Jesus, anything I took from ___ I send back, and anything ___ has taken from me or anything I have given to it, I now take back washed in the blood of Jesus.

By the authority and power of Jesus I bind the familiar spirit of ___ and cast it to Jesus' feet.

CHECK:
Father, does the familiar spirit of_____ have any hold over my life now?
If not free, ask **Why?** Then obey.

149

REPENT:
Father, what sinful patterns are in my life as a result of partnering with these familiar spirits? (ex. performance/self-protection, bitterness, fear, self-pity). *Father, am I willing to break partnership with these patterns?*

Holy Spirit, how can I cooperate with You to help me walk this out?

Father, forgive me for partnering with that familiar spirit of _____ and devaluing myself, who You have made me in Christ. Forgive me for not honoring who You, Father, say that I am. Father, do You forgive me? (Yes) *Then I forgive myself.*

EXCHANGE: *Father, what do You give me in exchange for _____ (each false identity)?*
Or: *Father, who do You say that I am?*

REJOICE: It is powerful for us to declare over ourselves the true identity we have received from the Father and rejoice in it. If you need to, ask Him for clarity on what that will look like in your life, or how you can cooperate with Him to live out who He has made you to be.

Once we are free from a false identity we may feel uncertain of how to act. If, for example, we were deceived into believing we are by nature insecure, instead of being confident of God's love, we may now feel vulnerable and uncertain as to how to conduct ourselves in certain situations, like when we walk into a crowded room. While this may make us uncomfortable because we like to be sure of ourselves, it is actually healthy for us to be aware of our dependence on

Jesus instead of charging ahead in self-confidence and independence, which, by the way, is highly prized in the world's eyes. This provides opportunity for us to turn to Him and respond to His lead. This is true maturity. So, as we walk into that crowded room, we can say: *Okay Jesus, I don't know how to do this but I'm trusting You and know You will help me.*

We simply do not know how to live the Christian life. Only Jesus does. He makes it clear: "Apart from Me you can do nothing" (John 15:5). Then, to underscore the fact, He declares that even "The Son can do nothing of Himself unless it is something He sees the Father doing" (John 5:19), modeling perfectly how we are to live in total dependence upon Him.

With confidence that the Father is eager to help us as we turn to Him and assured of the new identity He has spoken over us, rather than being hesitant and intimidated because of insecurity, we can anticipate His supernatural supply for every situation. We will find the Lord nudging us into actions that will break with old negative behaviors that crippled us before. He may lead us to reach out and serve others instead of being immobilized by our own sense of worthlessness. As we depend on who God says we are, despite any sense of vulnerability, we will discover the thrilling adventure and powerful opportunity for deeper intimacy and partnership with Him as we walk in our true identity.

CHAPTER 12

Temptation

*B*ill Johnson from Bethel Church in California told the story of two Christian men who were in financial difficulty. The two agreed to meet in a restaurant, but as they sat down at their table one of them noticed a large tip that had not been collected by the waiter. As the other excused himself to go to the restroom, the first guy was tempted to pocket the tip. It was a battle, but he left the tip on the table. When his friend returned from the restroom he noticed the tip and, without hesitation, called over the waiter and gave him the tip.

Both men had experienced similar circumstances but one trusted God to provide and the other was fearful. He had not taken those negative thoughts captive and processed them with God and was vulnerable to temptation.

Our hearts are made hungry for God, but if we don't turn to Him to meet our need we will be vulnerable to substitutes that will ultimately bring us into bondage. When our hearts are weakened through not receiving from and responding to Jesus, not only will substitutes have greater appeal, our ability to resist temptation will be severely limited.

> *As Jesus warns, an empty heart invites attack (Matthew 12:43-45).*

"God doesn't tempt anyone, but each one is tempted when he is carried away and enticed by his own lust" (James 1:13, 14). Those desires can be legitimate, initially anyway. We can be hungry, lonely, hurting. The appeal of temptation is that it offers to meet our need and bring us comfort. However, at its root, every temptation is a lie. Ultimately, it doesn't deliver what it offers. But, when we set our minds on the desires of our flesh–not taking negative and unclean thoughts captive–we are blinded to the deadly consequences of yielding to temptation.

Why are we drawn?

God makes it crystal clear. There is zero room for negotiation with our flesh. "Make no provision for the flesh in regard to its lusts" (Romans 13:14). But if all we do is summon our willpower to change our behavior without recognizing why we are pulled into destructive patterns, sooner or later we will end up discouraged, if not despairing. Painting over rotting lumber never works.

For example, we can try to overcome temptation to sexual lust by introducing computer blocks to pornography. We can have others hold us accountable. These attempts may be very helpful. However, if we do not deal with the root heart hunger, we will simply gravitate to another temptation.

> *We may overcome one temptation, but unless we address our heart condition we can easily adopt another idol to fill the vacancy.*

The question to ask the one who alone knows our hearts clearly is, "Father, *why* am I drawn …?" And let Him meet us there.

For instance, behind the attraction to pornography may be the need for validation, to feel wanted and appreciated or the desire for comfort and relief from pressure or pain or boredom. We are deceived into believing the lie that surrendering to temptation will meet our need, that it will satisfy us, comfort us, protect us, or give us control and power, when in fact it will ultimately leave us feeling dirty, empty, unfulfilled, and isolated.

The more we respond to the temptation, the more powerful the deception becomes and the more seared our conscience. We become addicted to the lie that our needs can be met, and we are blinded and callous to the devastation it causes, both to ourselves and to others.

He encourages us: "Listen carefully to Me and eat *[take it to heart]* what is good and delight yourself in abundance" (Isaiah 55:2b; emphasis added). Proactively giving the Father opportunity to speak and cooperating with Him, strengthens and fills the vulnerable, hungry places in our hearts and temptation loses its appeal. In fact, we become repulsed by it. The eyes of our heart are opened to the hollowness and deception behind the promise. Furthermore, He will also give us practical ways that are not beyond us, so we can follow His lead and find real freedom.

So, if God doesn't tempt anyone, why does Jesus encourage us to pray, "Lead us not into temptation" (Matthew 6:13). We have to live with the realization that we are always vulnerable to temptation so that we live, not in fear, but in dependence upon God.

The invitation

Maybe you already know this or think you do. Temptation is not sin. It's how we choose to respond to it that is the issue. After all, Jesus "has been tempted in all things as we are, yet without sin" (Hebrews 4:15). However, we still often act like temptation is sin, frequently beating ourselves up because we continue to be tempted. The enemy comes to us and says: *You are not free. You would not keep being tempted if you were really free.*

If we listen to the enemy and think God is disgusted by our vulnerability to temptation and repulsed by our weakness, we will pull away from Him. Instead, these weak places can actually be some of our greatest opportunities for intimacy with Him! The Father so longs for us to bring our struggles with temptation to Him. To come to Him, process our thoughts and feelings with Him, and then give Him the opportunity to counsel us, is His joy. This is where His kindness and power to redeem shines brightest.

A young woman came to Diane with a sincere desire to grow in her relationship with God, but was troubled by her impure thoughts. She was encouraged to ask the Father what He had to say to her about these thoughts. This is what she reported that He told her: *Offer each thought to me as a gift! It's my delight to meet you at the point of your greatest weakness and vulnerability because it can become the place of your deepest intimacy with me.*

The temptation to dodge taxes, to allow our eyes to wander, to avoid the truth and so on, may be all too familiar. Clearly, God allows us into situations so we will discover and recognize our weak and vulnerable places where there is any greed, lust, anger or fear so we will learn to turn to Him and overcome.

> *He is not out to see us exposed and defeated. He wants to strengthen us to win.*

After Jesus was led into the wilderness and overcame the enemy's temptations, He emerged in the power of the Spirit. This was His Father's intention all along. God intends no less for us.

Peter was sure he would not deny Jesus although Jesus told him he would. Peter's pride blinded him from what was really in his heart. Later, in the garden of Gethsemane, Jesus told him to watch and pray so that he would be able to resist temptation (Mark 14:38). But Peter fell asleep physically and spiritually. He had no idea of what was coming and how vulnerable he was. Jesus knew that this crisis was more than Peter could handle on his own. Jesus wants to speak to us about our vulnerable places to equip us and help us, so we are able to resist any onslaught.

If Peter had heeded Jesus' simple instructions to watch and pray, he could have avoided the greatest failure of his life. So, we need to be proactive in asking Jesus what He has for our hearts, so we are not blindsided and can overcome temptation. He knows what temptation feels like and longs for us to respond to the nudging of our helper, the Holy Spirit, so we can walk free.

Diane's escape

Even as a child, I (Diane) was an avid reader. Early on, I came across romance paperbacks. By the age of ten, I was addicted. It was a stronghold in my life for over three decades. I overcame it for long periods of time, but it would continue to tempt me, especially in times of stress. Part of the commitment I had made was that I would never go down the romance aisle of a bookstore.

While attending the Discipleship School of our local church, I felt the Lord prompt me to bring my spiritual language more to the forefront in my daily experience and to pray in tongues as much as possible. The Bible says that praying in the Holy Spirit is one way of building up our faith, our confidence in God (1 Corinthians 14:4; Jude 20). I had not been exercising that spiritual gift regularly and assumed the Lord was simply wanting to reawaken it in my life. So, I began quietly praying in tongues under my breath most of the day, no matter where I went. It kept my mind focused on the prompting of the Holy Spirit, whether in the grocery store praying for those around me or in any way He directed my thoughts.

It was a very busy time. The pace of the Discipleship School we were enrolled in was intense. My brother-in-law was dying of cancer. Our daughter was planning her wedding. Stress can easily make us vulnerable. The day came when I was going to meet a friend at the local Barnes and Noble bookstore. While waiting for her, I needed to go to the ladies' restroom and without thinking, I walked through the romance aisle. For an instant, I paused in my steps and turned, considering pulling a book off the shelf.

> *Suddenly, I was hit with a wave of nausea that almost doubled me over! Immediately, the Father spoke to me, quietly and firmly: Diane, I am so committed to your freedom!*

He knew when I would be vulnerable. He knew the temptation that would cross my path. And so, He had been faithfully helping me strengthen my spirit in preparation. He is so eager to partner with us, empower us and set us free.

Two necessary pillars of support

As we discussed in chapter 6, *Freedom from Lies,* the two primary accusations of the enemy are: God can't be trusted and there is something wrong with me. Strengthening our hearts by proactively receiving the truth in these two areas fortifies us against temptation. Without it, we are an easy target for the enemy.

First, to resist temptation we must be convinced that:

> *God is able and eager to*
> *meet me in my need.*

"…let us hold fast … for we do not have a high priest who cannot sympathize with our weaknesses, but one who has been tempted in all things as we are, yet without sin … *draw near with confidence … that we may receive mercy and may find grace to help in time of need*" (Hebrews 4:14-16; emphasis added).

"No temptation has overtaken you, but such as is common to man; and *God is faithful, who will not allow you to be tempted beyond* what you are able, but with the temptation will provide a way of escape … therefore, my beloved, flee from idolatry" (1 Corinthians 10:13, 14; emphasis added).

Not only did Jesus overcome every temptation, He is eager to give us the help we need when we are tempted. He doesn't just stand back ready to judge us if we blow it. When the pressure is on to cave in, we must be confident that He will deliver us when we turn to Him, otherwise we don't stand a chance. The more we turn to Him and receive what He has to say in exchange for the lies, the more we will be convinced of His desire and ability to meet our hearts. Furthermore, as Jan Johnson says: "As we get to know the heart of God, we're more likely to refuse temptation because we love God too much to give in." (*When the Soul Listens, p.141*).

Second, to resist temptation we must be convinced that:

> *temptation does not appeal to my true self.*
> *To sin is unnatural to me!*

In the previous chapter on False Identities, we laid the biblical foundation for the confidence we can enjoy of having the Father's DNA as brand-new creations in Christ. We explained how walking in the reality of who the Father says we are will give us a tremendous advantage in rejecting sin and responding to God. Now, let us look a little closer at how this applies in the area of temptation.

We may understand that temptation itself is not sin, but when we are tempted, especially if frequently in the same area, we are prone to believe the lie that there is something inherently wrong with me. I am, by nature, weak and vulnerable in this area. I will never be free. I am stuck. Accepting these lies results in condemnation and shame and the loss of the will to stand and resist the enemy's seduction.

Understand this: Jesus had to be vulnerable to be truly tempted. But being tempted did not mean He was, by nature, weak. Because He was tempted in all things (Hebrews 4:15) as we are, it is clear that Jesus would have been tempted to fear and lust, for example. Does that mean the Jesus was, by nature, a fearful or lustful person? Of course not! Neither then, does temptation say anything about our nature, our true identity in Christ.

The Scripture is perfectly clear:

> "… we who died to sin … buried with Him … our old self was crucified with Him … no longer slaves to sin ... he who has died is freed from sin … consider yourselves dead to sin and alive to God" (Romans 6:1-11).

This is not a mind game or an attempt at positive thinking. This is our reality and it is huge! To consider ourselves dead to sin and alive to God, we must first know it. Do we? Previously, Romans 6:6 says: "Knowing that our old self was crucified with Christ." Remember, nothing comes down alive from the cross! If you are unsure, ask God for revelation so you can be certain, and then you can "consider" your old self dead–with confidence.

Peter boldly declares: "He has … granted to us everything pertaining to life and godliness … precious and magnificent promises in order that you might become partakers of the divine nature, having escaped the corruption that is in the world by lust" (2 Peter 1:3, 4). Lust, fear or anger are no longer in our true nature.

Nevertheless, we are frequently reminded in Scripture to stay alert and resist the pull of the flesh and the devil. "… the Spirit of Him who raised Jesus from the dead dwells in you … we are under obligation, not to the flesh … by the Spirit, putting to death the deeds of the body ...." (Romans 8:11-13). So, we are exhorted to continue to choose, in the face of temptation, to put to death, to stand on the ground of Christ's finished work in shattering the power of our flesh.

We have every reason to rejoice in the freedom He has won for us. "For you have not received a spirit of slavery leading to fear again but you have received a spirit of adoption as sons by which we cry out 'Abba Father!' ... we are children of God" (Romans 8:15-16).

> *We are born from above. Hear it again. We have our heavenly Father's DNA!*

How we see ourselves, who we are convinced we really are, is vital if we are not to be shaken by temptation.

Beware of the stronghold

When we believe lies and give into temptation, we give the enemy right of access and a foothold, making it easy for him to traffic with us and tempt us further. We may need to:
1) renounce the lie that gave the enemy a foothold and
2) break off a demonic spirit (such as lust, anger, fear, etc.) especially if we find our willpower is insufficient to bring change.

If we continue to give into temptation, we reinforce a demonic bond and come to believe the lie that I am, in fact, a lustful person, or an angry person, or an anxious person. Or that I'm lazy, broken, dirty, worthless, inadequate, driven. This is how I actually am. This is natural to me. These lies, or false identities can lead us to feel that resistance is hopeless.

> *If we believe a lie about who we are, we will live out of that stronghold!*

As we ask the Father, He will bring to light the lies and assumptions about the nature of God and ourselves that set us up for temptation, such as: God is not enough, I am weak, and this is what I need, etc.

To sum up then, our ability to resist temptation will depend upon:

1) our confidence in Jesus to meet with us in our places of greatest weakness, to fill our hearts and satisfy the deepest root of our need in the moment of temptation, and

2) confidence in the radically new, righteous person God has made us to be who is well able, by the unlimited power of the indwelling Holy Spirit, to resist every appeal of the enemy.

Such confidence comes from receiving His words of life, particularly in those two areas, and embracing them in our hearts.

JOURNAL ON TEMPTATION

Ask the Lord where we are vulnerable to temptation and how we can cooperate with Him to overcome.

Jesus, what are the most vulnerable areas of temptation in my life?
   What do You have to say to me about these temptations?

What patterns of sin reoccur when I'm under pressure?
   What steps do You want me to take about this?

Jesus, what proactive strategy do You want me to put in place, so I am not blindsided by temptation?

What am I willing to do?
Perhaps ...

- offer the temptation to Him as a gift and ask Him for an exchange
- find someone you can trust to hold you accountable and pray together
- wait on Him together to receive fresh insight and a practical strategy
- open the door through worship for fresh perspective and allow Him to strengthen your spirit

Jesus, when I react in my flesh …
How do You want me to respond to You?
Or, *What steps do You want me to take?* (Make a plan. Share it)

Is there anything I am keeping hidden?
Why am I hiding it? What do You want me to do about it?
How do You want me to stand against this temptation?

Any time you give in to temptation, ask Jesus:

What am I believing right now?

What do You want to say to me?

Don't forget that He always wants to help, not condemn.

CHAPTER 13

Sexual Sin

*I*t doesn't take any discernment to recognize that sexual sin is not only excused but advocated and promoted like never before.

Perhaps in no other arena has the enemy's strategy brought such havoc and bondage. With the breakdown of a moral compass has come escalating degrees of wounding, some of the deepest we can experience, whether we have violated ourselves or others, or whether we have been violated.

This is where the enemy often finds fertile ground to sow his lies against the trustworthiness of the Father and our value to Him. The result has been lack of confidence in God and increasing levels of self-hatred and shame. Struggles with sexual identity and gender confusion abound.

In the face of this deluge, how absolutely wonderful it is that Jesus came to redeem and heal us, thoroughly and completely. He has made a way, no matter the depth of our pain or captivity. Just as the sheep that is stuck cries out to the good Shepherd, so He delights in rescuing us and carrying us home to safety and wholeness.

Although sometimes very difficult, the path to freedom is often quite simple.

After David's adultery with Bathsheba, he recognized that his sin was, first, against God Himself. "Against You and You only have I sinned" (Psalm 51:4). He didn't trust God to give him what he needed so he sought to gratify himself. This was Eve's sin (Genesis 3:4, 5), believing the accuser's lie that God was withholding what was best for her. Doubting the Father's heart for us is ultimately always how the enemy attacks, and we must repent for any agreement with him.

Before we continue, I must say that I am continually struck by the Father's readiness to forgive our sin (Psalm 86:5), especially when there has been a long history of rebellion that has had even devastating consequences upon others. The key, of course, is that our repentance must come from the heart, and He is the only one who sees our hearts clearly. This scripture should be enough to sober us all: "There is no creature that is not manifest in His sight, but all things are naked and laid open before the eyes of Him with whom we have to do" (Hebrews 4:13).

When listening to God, as we have said, if we are not really open and yielded to whatever He has to say, we can hear what we want to hear. If we have avoided facing our sin, we may be inclined to think that God will overlook it too. The fact is that if we continue sowing to the flesh, we will reap the consequences and so will others. If you have any inclination to minimize the impact of pornography, for instance, we encourage you to turn now to the article at the end of this chapter before continuing. Unless we hate our sin, we will never leave it. However, to the one who is honest, open and surrendered, according to the light they have, His grace to meet us there is breathtaking.

Only when we have first received the Father's forgiveness, can we effectively forgive ourselves. Genuinely forgiving others may be much more difficult, as we addressed in Chapter 7, but this is the necessary beginning on the road to freedom and healing.

When sinned against

More than a decade ago, Diane was in a group of Christian women who were asked whether they had been molested or sexually violated in some way. All were shocked when ten of the thirteen raised their hands. Since that time, she has seen a consistent pattern in Listening Prayer* sessions with hundreds of women, where the majority has experienced some form of sexual violation.

If we have been abused, this may have resulted in lies we believe about God or ourselves which is lie-based pain. However, there is also pain that is truth-based, as we discussed in the chapter on Processing Grief and Loss. This truth-based pain can, for example, be the result of the loss of innocence or the betrayal of those who should have protected us.

As part of the healing process, it is necessary to name the abuse for what it is. It is stunning how the abused so frequently believe the accusations of the enemy that it was their fault, that there was something wrong with them. It is also very helpful to name the abuser, if possible, so we can effectively forgive.

*** Footnote:**

Listening Prayer is now a term used by a variety of ministries, often with different meanings. The ministry that the Lord has developed through us, after having received widely from the body of Christ, is simply where we facilitate a person in a sustained conversation with God, so they might encounter Him and, if needed, overcome hindrances to intimacy. Our goal is to equip the person to draw directly from God as their primary source.

So, we must renounce any lies we have believed that the Holy Spirit reveals of God or self. But then, we come before God, bring our pain before Him and grieve the losses.

The following *Renunciation of Sexual Sin* will guide you through this cleansing process. As always, it is critical that we genuinely engage our hearts as we work through it. Before jumping into the *Renunciation of Sexual Sin,* it may be helpful to introduce 'The Box'.

The Box

This tool, which we first learned from the SOZO ministry (Bethel Church, Redding, California), can be very helpful in vividly illustrating, through the use of sanctified imagination, Jesus' authority and victory on our behalf in dealing with sin and its effect on our hearts. We have found it particularly useful when dealing with many related sins, (either our own or by others against us) such as immoral relationships and pornographic exposure that are part of a perverted sexual history.

We may ask Jesus to show us a picture of a box. Then we may ask Him to 'place' the related issues of sin, unhealthy relationships and so on, into the box as the Holy Spirit brings them to mind.

Next, we deal with the contents of the box, the sin, through repentance, forgiveness, and renunciation or whatever is appropriate, and receive cleansing, deliverance and forgiveness. We may use the *Renunciation of Sexual Sin* below to accomplish this.

At the end of the *Renunciation,* we give the box to Jesus and ask Him what he is going to do with it.

167

————————❋————————

Renunciation of Sexual Sin

IF THE BOX IS USED: *Jesus, I ask You to give me a visual representation of a box.*

IDENTIFY: *Holy Spirit, I ask You to bring to my mind those sexual uses of my body as an instrument of unrighteousness, both those sins I have committed, and those sins committed against me, so that Jesus can 'put' them into this box.*

Ask Jesus to 'place' sexual encounters, relationships, images, etc. in the box as they come to mind.

REPENT: *Father, am I willing to truly repent of my sexual sin?* If willing, then proceed.
If not, ask God for His perspective, such as:

Father, what do You want me to know so that I will hate this sin and want to turn from it?

How does my sin affect my relationship with You?

How does my sin impact others and myself?

Father, I repent for all the ways I have used, violated and wounded others (identify) *and myself by turning my back on You and seeking to gratify myself. I repent for joining with the enemy and deliberately choosing to use my body as an instrument of unrighteousness.*

Father, I confess my sexual sin to You and ask You to forgive me and wash me clean. Father, do You forgive me? (Yes)

Thank You, Father, for the blood of Jesus, for the terrible price You paid so I can be forgiven! I forgive myself.

IF SINNED AGAINST – FORGIVE:
*Father, am I willing to forgive (*identify*) for sinning against me? (*then*) Father, I forgive (*identify*) for using me to gratify their own lust. I forgive them for violating me and exposing me to their sin.*

I release them from any anger, bitterness, resentment, judgment or expectations and commit them into Your hands. I ask You to pursue them with Your grace, open their eyes to Your love and mercy and speak the truth to them so they can be free.
I bless them in Jesus' name.

REJECT LIE: *Because of the blood of Jesus shed for me, I reject the devil's lie that my body is dirty, or in any way unacceptable to You as a result of my past sexual experiences.*

REJOICE IN TRUTH: *Father, thank You that You have totally cleansed me and forgiven me and that You love and accept me just the way I am. Therefore, I choose to accept myself and my body as clean in Your eyes. Thank You, Father!*

COMMIT: *I choose now to present my whole body – my eyes, mouth, mind, heart, hands and sexual organs – to You as an instrument of righteousness and I choose to reserve the sexual use of my body for marriage only.*

FOLLOW THROUGH: *Father, is there any action You want me to take*
   1) *towards those I have violated?*
   2) *to walk in purity?*

Am I willing to obey You in this?

IF THE BOX WAS USED:

We give the box and its contents to Jesus and ask Him what He wants to do with it. He may give us a vivid visual of Him removing or destroying the box (ex. Micah 7:19b).

We may then ask: *Jesus, what has happened to the power of the contents of the box in my life?*

Thank Him!

Then ask: Jesus, what do You want to give me in exchange? *Receive what He says by declaring it and rejoicing.*

The Impact of Pornography

While this is addressed to men, clearly women are increasingly lured into this trap.

A 7-year-old caught her dad, a missionary, watching pornography and masturbating. Embarrassed, he burst out in anger against her. She didn't understand but felt violated and so distanced herself from her father and ever since has experienced no closeness with him. Now herself a missionary, she has had difficulty enjoying intimacy with her husband. The appeal of the purity of godly, marital sex was destroyed by exposure to perversion. Thankfully, our Redeemer is restoring the years the locusts had eaten.

1. Pornography opens the door to demonic spirits such as lust, perversion, violation, sensuality, objectification and shame.
2. Demonic strongholds result in crippling bondage. Freedom of choice is lost as lust is never satisfied and perversion deepens leading to addictions, lack of self-control, lying, hiddenness, deceit, adultery and

exploitation. Often pornographic images are of victims of sex trafficking.

3. As head of the home, a father's covering is compromised, and the family is more vulnerable to the enemy's inroads. Many guys have shared with me (Rick) that they were led into their addiction to pornography because of their dad's example or finding his stash of magazines.

4. Rapists, pedophiles, instigators of incest, etc., very often began with exposure to pornography. Ted Bundy, the notorious serial rapist and killer, confessed on death row that it all started with porn.

5. Sex is primarily spiritual. You lose part of yourself with every unholy encounter.

6. Sexual addiction does not disappear with marriage.

7. Indulgence in fantasy distorts reality and can result, over time, in a husband's dysfunction with his wife.

8. A husband who views pornography dishonors his wife. She feels a deep sense of betrayal, violation, and perhaps of worthlessness, that she will never measure up, that she can't compete. The resulting insecurity can produce lack of abandonment to her husband and cause her to withdraw and shut down emotionally.

9. Because of his addiction, through fear of lust, a father may pull back and distance himself from his daughter when she matures. Wives may fear to fully trust their husbands with their daughters.

A high-school girl close to her dad, a believer, caught him watching porn and felt violated, slimed and self-conscious. She couldn't trust the way her dad or brother looked at her. She lost the sense of her own value believing the lie, *That's all I'm good for. That's how I can be valued and wanted.* So, she began to seek attention from guys and enter into pro-miscuous relationships.

If you don't hate what pornography does, you will never turn from it. In the section on Renunciation for Sexual Sin there are some suggested questions to ask God to help here. However, there are many who hate what it does to them-selves and others, yet still feel trapped. If this is true of you, you may find it helpful to return to Chapter 8 on Demolishing Spiritual Strongholds.

Although our bondages can be deeply ingrained over many years, Jesus died to set us free. There is absolutely no need for us to settle for anything less.

CHAPTER 14

Orphan Spirit

*R*elatively few of us in the Western world are orphans, so we may be inclined to write this chapter off as applicable to someone else. However, we have found this false identity so incredibly common that we felt we had to address it.

Take Jack. He came from a well-to-do family. His Dad was a successful businessman, but his work was demanding and stressful, and he had little left over for his family. Sure, he would try to get to some of Jack's baseball games, but he was mostly preoccupied and rarely asked him how he was doing or really listened to Jack if he ever tried to share his heart. With five siblings, his stay-at-home Mom constantly battled with chaos and depression, looking to Jack as the oldest to support her emotionally. Jack grew up feeling he was responsible to keep the peace and maintain order. He felt abandoned and alone, that no one understood the demands he was struggling with, and no one had the emotional capacity to take care of him.

If, because of our history, we feel we haven't had a safe place to share our fears and struggles, then we can be vulnerable to the enemy's attacks to question the character of God which often leads to questions about our identity and value.

tentacles of an octopus, a variety of strongholds, aps false identities, can spring from an orphan spirit.

p down, I believe that I cannot depend upon God to take care of me, that I cannot trust in His kindness, then doors are easily opened to many forms of bondage. I may believe that I am not known, understood, valued, wanted, pursued, supported, protected, defended, comforted, encouraged—not loved by the Father in the way I need.

As a consequence, I may feel I need to take care of myself, to be self-reliant and independent. If there is a problem, I had better fix it. If there is a need, I had better take care of it. I put pressure on myself to make things happen. I can't trust God, and maybe anyone else, so I can't relax. Perhaps I feel compelled to be in control. I'm not free to be a kid. There's no time to let down, play and have fun. I live with pressure and stress. Because I don't feel valued, I will search for and strive to find it. Because we are created for intimacy, we will never be satisfied without it. As a result, I may perform for approval. I may manipulate for affection. This is often the reason many seek inappropriate sexual relationships.

If I mess up, I may have little confidence that I can come to my heavenly Father for encouragement, but rather expect a frown of disapproval and disappointment, a correction, or even rejection. Even if I try my best, I never feel like it's enough to please Him. I'm not so sure that the Father enjoys me, that He is that interested in me, that He has time for me, so I feel like an interruption, an imposition, a nuisance, a problem, a burden. I'm intimidated, reluctant to approach Him, even if it's just to spend time with Him.

I may feel that I will always miss out, that life will be a struggle, that I can only hope to just scrape by, that I will never receive what I need. Those scriptures that speak about abundance

must be for someone else. I don't trust the Father to be kind and generous with me. This is called a poverty mentality.

> *It all adds up to feeling deep down, alone, abandoned and unwanted.*

I love these images from *Moving Mountains* by John Eldredge:

> *"You are not an orphaned child, sitting in the hall hoping your busy Father will see one of the notes you have pushed under his door … you are not a homeless beggar standing on the corner hoping God will pass by … you are not the refugee standing in line at the embassy. Not even the faithful servant, humbly trying to do your best."*

Hear afresh the Father's heart over you:

> I will not leave you as orphans; I will come to you (John 14:18).

> You have not received a spirit of slavery leading to fear again, but you have received a spirit of adoption as sons by which we cry out, "Abba! Father!" (Romans 8:15).

> He predestined us to adoption as sons through Jesus Christ to Himself, according to the kind intention of His will (Ephesians 1:5).

We encourage you to do the following exercise and hear from the Father if you have allowed this orphan spirit to have access to your heart and rob you of intimacy with Him.

Orphan Spirit Renunciation

An orphan spirit is often manifested by a persistent theme of feeling abandoned, alone, unwanted, or not cared for; where we feel we must take care of ourselves.

You may find it necessary to ask the Father if there is any parent you need to forgive before proceeding further. If so, return to the journaling exercise in Chapter 7 on Forgiveness.

Father, have I opened myself to an orphan spirit?

Am I ready to break with that orphan spirit?
If not, you may ask Him what He requires first.

BREAK OFF:
I renounce and break off all influence, agreement and authority I have given to an orphan spirit that would cause me to feel I am alone and that I cannot rely on You Father to help me or depend on Your love for me. By the authority and power of Jesus I break off all soul ties and any way in which I have taken on 'orphan' as my identity. I bind the orphan spirit by the authority and power of Jesus and cast it to His feet.

REPENT:
Father, I repent for partnering with that orphan spirit, for not believing in Your love for me, for believing that You would abandon me and leave me alone. Father, do You forgive me? (Yes) Then I forgive myself.

RECEIVE:
Father, I receive the Spirit of adoption that Y
ised me according to your Word so that my w
cry "Abba Father."
Father, who do You say that I am?

REJOICE:
Declare and rejoice in the identity the Father speaks over you!
Ask: *Father, what does it mean to You that I am your son/daughter?*

What do You want it to mean to me that You are my Father?
Father, what do You enjoy about me?

Make these Declarations aloud!

Father, I rejoice that You chose me because You wanted me!

I rejoice that You will never leave me alone; that You are totally committed to helping me and taking care of me!

Father, I rejoice that You are absolutely trustworthy, dependable and faithful!

I rejoice that I can run to You with a humble heart, no matter how I have messed up, confident of Your embrace and delight, with no fear of rejection!

Father, I rejoice that I am secure in Your unconditional love!

I rejoice in Your grace lavished on me as Your beloved son/daughter!

CHAPTER 15

Self-Hatred and Shame

*S*elf-hatred is so prevalent that it is, in our experience, until addressed, almost a universal area of bondage, believers included. At first we may react to the inference that we may personally struggle in this area. After all, it does sound a little dramatic. Good grief! I don't *hate* myself! Of course, I have issues. Who doesn't? But it's not *that* bad.

Self-hatred or self-condemnation is one of the most common and destructive works of the enemy. The Holy Spirit calls him "the accuser of the brethren" (Revelation 12:10). In fact, as we mentioned in Chapter 6, the enemy, in every Old Testament reference bar one (1 Chronicles 21:1) is literally called, not Satan, but the Accuser. Agreeing with the enemy, beating ourselves up or seeing ourselves as worthless is so widespread among believers that I (Rick) am surprised in those rare cases where I come across someone who has *not* lost some ground to the enemy here.

Clearly, when we sin we give the enemy ammunition to accuse us, but once we confess and repent, he has no grounds for accusation and we can stand secure, justified by the blood of Jesus. However, we all have ongoing struggles where we don't respond to the Lord as wholeheartedly as we should and so it is easy to fall into discouragement and become susceptible to the enemy's condemnation and lies.

Men commonly come under the pressure to achieve and often tend to struggle with feeling inadequate and not having what it takes. Women have the pressure to be attractive, so they may be prone to believing they are unwanted and not valued.

Some years ago, a man asked if I could facilitate Listening Prayer for him. He was a tall, imposing, well-dressed guy who was successful in business and who, at first glance, seemed confident and self-assured, even intimidating. I posed a question for him to ask the Father: *When I look inside myself, what do I see?* He began to shake and finally whispered: *Trash!* Beneath his impressive appearance, he was struggling to compensate for the deeply ingrained conviction that he was worthless. He knew what the Father revealed was true although he had never, until then, faced the fact that he believed this lie.

I punished myself for most of my life, but I didn't see it as a negative thing. I thought I was doing God a favor. I was policing myself. *Rick, what are you doing? Don't get proud now. Humble yourself.* While I thought it was a good thing, it was robbing me of joy. Of course, by trying to keep myself humble I was focusing on myself, attempting to project an image, to change myself and make myself acceptable. I was trying to be my own savior. It was false humility–simply, pride. I didn't really believe I was destitute. I was seeking my own righteousness, thereby discounting the gift of God's righteousness through Jesus. For this reason, it's not uncommon for zealous believers to actually be reluctant to break with any spirit of self-hatred.

As Jan Johnson articulates, instead of trying to be good, we connect with God to let God transform us into

179

Christlikeness. As we do the connecting with God, God does the perfecting in us.

Being angry with one's self never works. James 1:20 nails it. "The anger of man does not achieve the righteousness of God."

The power behind these accusations of worthlessness point to what could be called a punishing or a self-condemning spirit. Partnering with this demonic spirit has particularly devastating consequences.

> *Primarily, it hinders or even prevents us from receiving the love of God.*

Of course, this is exactly the design of the enemy, but we rarely recognize it because we are so used to it. God may tell us all day: *I love you! I'm proud of you!* We may respond: *Thank You, Lord. I appreciate that. However, ...* and we turn inward, see our failures, and what the Father has spoken simply bounces off. Inevitably, our hearts remain largely untouched.

All too often our response to His affirmation is, *Thank You, Father but I am still dealing with issues that I should have overcome by now.* If *we* think we are not doing well, then it's easy to assume that *God*, who is holy and perfect, must be far more disappointed in us. Self-condemnation makes it very difficult for us to really believe anything affirming or encouraging that God has to say about us.

On the cross, Jesus took *all* the punishment due us. He declared: *It is finished!* However, by beating ourselves up we are, in effect, denying that He took all the punishment for us and that we deserve more. We may not have ever thought of it that way, but that's the reality. *Thanks for what You did for me Jesus, but it wasn't enough.* We negate the power of what He accomplished for us on the cross by punishing ourselves. This leaves us wide open to agreeing with the enemy's accusations and condemnation.

The Bible says that as we repent, the blood of Jesus covers our sin, that He forgives us, that our sin is removed from us as far as the East is from the West, so there is no condemnation for those who are in Christ Jesus (Romans 8:1) and the enemy has no ground to stand on.

Watchman Nee points out in *The Normal Christian Life*, that it was *when God saw the blood* on the doorposts of the homes of the children of Israel held captive in Egypt, the angel of death passed over them (Exodus 12:23). When we repent and come under the covering of the blood of Jesus on our behalf, God is completely satisfied, and we are justified in His sight–whether we feel it or fully appreciate it or not. The blood Jesus shed was first for God to see–not us!

Personally, because self-hatred crippled me much of my life, I couldn't really believe that God loved me as I was, unconditionally, without me changing, without me doing anything. It was a real stretch to believe He fully accepted me. So, when He told me how delighted He was in me, it wasn't easy to digest at first, because for so many years I had listened to critical voices that put me down, and I guess I expected Him to do the same. To love ourselves as God does, we must see ourselves through His eyes. Here again, asking Him and listening to how He sees us can bring us joy like we have never known!

Self-hatred has another major consequence.

> *We have difficulty receiving the love*
> *and affirmation of others.*

Any time I was affirmed I would feel awkward. I felt that if I received it, I was being proud. Years ago, I was speaking in a Discipleship School, and I was introduced by a sweet, young lady who generously affirmed me as a brother in Christ. I thought to myself that this was terrible. Surely, only God should get any glory. I was embarrassed. I thought by refusing to receive this affirmation that I was being humble and righteous. I didn't acknowledge the students' applause or thank them for it. I soon realized that something in me was off. As I was talking to the Father about this afterward, He said: *Rick, you do the same with me! I encourage you. I affirm you. But you don't receive it!*

Henri Nouwen described his experience: "How quickly we give in to this temptation of self-rejection. For example, I remember speaking to thousands of people, and many would say, "That was wonderful, what you said." But, if one person stood up to say, "Hey, I thought that was a lot of nonsense," that was the only person I would remember." *(Spiritual Direction, p.30)*

Finally, Jesus said we are to love our neighbors as ourselves, but

> *if we are relentlessly critical of ourselves,*
> *we will be judgmental of others.*

If we are inclined to focus on where we feel we are lacking, then we will tend to look at others through that same filter and gravitate to what we think is wrong with them. We may not tell the person, but we may think: *Why don't you get your act together. What's your problem?* Sometimes, even without saying anything, a person can pick up our judgmental vibes and feel condemned or less than, around us. We cannot love others well if we don't like the way God has made us.

Common Evidence of Self-Hatred

Any time we want clarity on what is going on in our hearts, we need to ask the Father because we don't see ourselves clearly, as we mentioned at the beginning of this chapter. As for myself, if I had been asked if I dealt with self-hatred, I would have denied it without hesitation, thinking, *of course I mess up, but I don't hate myself!* Self-condemnation is a little easier to admit.

Do not analyze and self-examine, instead – ask:

Father, do You see evidence of this in my life? (His conviction is never accusing or condemning).

- Performance - striving, perfectionism.
- Comparison - jealousy, self-pity, defensive-ness, rejection
- Criticism, judgment and condemnation of others_
- Unworthiness – I'm not worthy to receive what God has for me.
- Hopelessness, depression – the deepest root of depression is "There is nothing in me worth loving" – depression is anger turned inward, against yourself.
- Addictions, cutting – attempts to numb pain of self-hatred
- Difficulty receiving affirmation – false humility.
- Tending to be negative about yourself: I'm worthless. There's something wrong with me. I'm never going to make it. I'm not enough. I don't have what it takes. God's angry with me or at least disappointed in me.

These negative flesh patterns are viral, like bacteria. Why? Simply because the enemy does not want us to know how much God cares about us and self-condemnation stops us from receiving His heart for us.

We may need to forgive others for leading us to feel worthless and opening the door to self-hatred. If there is a sin issue, we will need to repent. We need to receive the Father's forgiveness, otherwise it will be very easy for the enemy to point to our failures, accuse us and lead us to feel condemned. Remember that the conviction of the Holy Spirit will always motivate us to come back to the Father and be reconciled.

We may also need to break off a spirit of self-hatred or self-condemnation in Jesus' name. This is the power behind the lie that we have agreed with. Remember that when we agree with a lie, we are partnering with the enemy and giving him legal right of access that gives him opportunity to establish a demonic stronghold. Years ago, after seeing many guys break off the spirit of self-hatred, I began to wonder what practical difference it was making in their lives. How effective was this?

That's when the Father showed me that I myself had been dealing with this stronghold most of my life. When I broke with that spirit of self-hatred, it was as if I was coming out of a fog that I had lived in nearly all of my life and I thought: *What on earth have I been doing?* Because I was so used to kicking myself, and I had dug such a deep trench for so long, I wondered whether I could really get out and get free. I asked the Holy Spirit that any time I was tempted to whack myself, condemn myself or give access to these demonic lies, that He would stop me in my tracks and show me. As I listened, He said He would. Since then, I have been absolutely amazed at His faithfulness in alerting me, after all the years where I had become desensitized, so that He has kept me from stumbling. The deception was exposed, and I have been able to reject the enemy's scheme and turn and receive the truth my heart needed from the Father.

Truly, the Holy Spirit is the helper that Jesus proi. didn't say: *Well, you are on your own now. You've been m* up but now I've cleaned you up so off you go and behave. course, without Him there is no way to really change. No. He says: *Stick with Me. I'm going to help you do this.* Hand in hand with Him we can walk free from any addiction or stronghold no matter how long we have been imprisoned by it.

Only when we receive forgiveness from God can we truly forgive ourselves. We have to know we are fully accepted by God in Christ before we can fully accept ourselves. This is why listening to the Father and receiving from Him is so life-transforming.

If we don't know that we are accepted by Him, we will seek validation from others. But, of course, that will never be enough, and we will always end up wounded and disappointed. Remember, that it is not the treatment or the choices of others that define us, unless we agree with them. Any father or mother wound does not define us. The identity that the Father speaks over us is what defines us, but we have to receive it. That's why we need to hear from Him again and again what He has to say about us.

Journal and Renunciation of Self-Hatred

JOURNAL

Father, am I able to fully receive your unconditional love? (If not) *Father, do I walk in a pattern of condemning myself?* (If yes) Father, *is there anything I need to repent of that I'm holding against myself?* (You may first need to address any

area of sin that arises by repenting and receiving His forgiveness before proceeding further.)

*Father, is there anyone I need to forgive who has caused
me to believe lies about myself?* (if needed, use Steps to
Forgiveness in Chapter 7)

*Father, do I need to break with a punishing and condemning
spirit?* (if so, proceed).

Am I willing to break with this spirit? (If not) *Father, what will
my life be like if I do break with this spirit?*

What will my life be like if I don't break with this spirit?

(Or) *Father, what do I believe this spirit is doing for me?*

What do You have to say about that?"

RENUNCIATION

Repent: *Father forgive me for believing the lie that Jesus'
sacrifice was not enough to make me righteous in Your eyes.
I repent for not accepting Your forgiveness. Forgive me for
not receiving Your love. Father forgive me for believing I
need to win Your approval. Forgive me for trying to change
myself and not trusting Jesus to change me. Forgive me for
not admitting I am destitute without You, for seeking my own
righteousness and not Yours.*

*Father, I ask your forgiveness for partnering with that pun-
ishing spirit and condemning myself. Forgive me for devaluing myself-the new person You have made me to be.*

Forgive me for grieving You by being harsh with myself, for being impatient and frustrated with myself, for not giving myself room to fail, and not loving myself as You love me.

Father, do You forgive me? (Yes) *Then, as You have forgiven me, I forgive myself.*

Renounce: *Father, I renounce and break off all influence, agreement and authority I have given to a spirit of self-hatred that led me to believe I must condemn myself for what is already covered by the blood of Jesus. By the authority and power of Jesus I bind that spirit of self-hatred and cast it to His feet.*

Receive: *Father, what do You have for me in exchange for self-hatred?* (Or) *Father, what do You have for me in exchange for the lie I have believed about myself?*

Thank Him, declare it and **Rejoice!**

Shame

For simplicity's sake, we will make a distinction between shame and conviction. We will assume shame is always unhealthy. Conviction, on the other hand, is a wonderful gift.

When we make sinful choices or bad things are done to us, we may feel shame as a result. The conviction of the Holy Spirit is His kind intervention to bring us to repentance and receive forgiveness, cleansing and restoration. Shame, however, is used by the accuser to turn us inward and cut us off from the grace of God.

Shame is a very effective tool of the enemy that is rampant in the church and is particularly common in the area of sexual sin and addictions. When we blow it, the accuser often comes as the "angel of light" seeming oh so spiritual and says something like: *How could you do something like that, after all the ways God has loved you and been so faithful to you? You are still dealing with that stuff and you call yourself a believer? You should be beyond that by now.*

All too often our response is: *Absolutely! That was terrible. How stupid! What was I thinking? What an idiot!*

> *We often embrace shame and the accusations and condemnation of the enemy, thinking that if we feel badly enough about our sin or failure it will strengthen our resolve to not do it again.*
>
> *But that's a trap.*

If we feel enough shame and really hate this thing, we will stop doing it.

Furthermore, we can be put under shame by others, where we are sinned against, as in humiliation and abuse. All too often, when someone has been violated, they succumb to the lie and the accompanying shame, that this is all they are good for. Tragically, this then keeps them vulnerable to further abuse, which the enemy will take advantage of.

By accepting the enemy's accusations, we are actually embracing shame. As we cling to our shame, we pull back from God assuming that if we think it's bad, then He must be totally disgusted with us. As we turn away from Him, we start to feel even more hopeless because God is the source of our hope. We feel so badly about what we've done, we may begin to think: *Well, what's the use, I'm such a mess. I've gone this far, what difference will it make now?* Shame not only undermines our resolve to stop, it propels us back into the very thing we are trying to get free from.

I think of those who are suffering as a result of substance abuse and live on the streets in our city. I guess many of the older ones would be struggling with shame as a result of walking away from responsibilities to family and children. Does shame ever propel them to go back and reconcile with their families and try and put things right? Rarely. All too often it drives them back into their addictions. Likewise, we as believers are vulnerable to the same cycle.

> *Shame condemns us to sin again and again.*

After years of struggling with pornography and masturbation, Joe, a new missionary, finally confessed to the guys on his team. He was propelled into this addiction seeking comfort because of feeling alone and unknown. He believed for years, that if it became known that he had this struggle that he would be rejected, so he kept it hidden. Stuck in fear and shame, he kept people at a distance, which reinforced his desire for comfort and his vulnerability to pornography, perpetuating the vicious cycle. As it turned out, rather than rejection, Joe's mature team embraced him, and his healing and freedom could begin.

A pedophile was asked: *Where would you be without your shame?* He replied: *In hell!* He was holding onto his shame to try and keep himself from sinning and to try and pay for his sin. This is where shame is closely linked with self-condemnation.

After their sin, Adam and Eve tried to hide from God, and covered themselves with fig leaves. Shame causes us to pull back from God and do things to try and feel better about ourselves or look okay to others. But God didn't leave Adam and Eve to themselves. He called out to them. He is always pursuing us. He wanted restoration. He killed an animal and covered them with the skin, a beautiful picture of how Jesus would later be the sacrifice who would bear the shame of us all, so we can come out from hiding, own our sin, but then be covered by his complete forgiveness.

Jesus paid fully for our failure. He not only forgives us our sin as we repent, but He also bore the pain, grief and sorrow we experience over our sin in His own body on the cross, so we don't need to carry the weight of guilt and shame any more. What a redeemer!

To walk free from shame, we may also need to break with any demonic *spirit* of shame that we have become attached to, if that is what God reveals to us.

We must come to Jesus in total honesty and vulnerability and pour out our hearts—our feelings about our sin—and give them to Him. Then, and only then, will we be able to receive His love and peace.

If we are really free from shame, we won't be like the prodigal son, as we mentioned earlier, who was probably dragging his feet with his head down on his way back home. Once we have repented from the heart, we are free to run into our Father's embrace, confident of his full acceptance and joy over us because everything has been paid for by Jesus.

We encourage you to walk through the following with Jesus.

Shame - Renunciation

Shame is a very effective tool of the enemy that is rampant in the church. The enemy often comes as an angel of light (2 Corinthians 11:14) to make us feel awful, either for what we did (our sin) or what was done to us.

All too frequently we embrace shame and the accusations and condemnation of the enemy, thinking that if we feel badly enough about our sin it will strengthen our resolve to not sin again.

However, the opposite is true. Shame causes us to pull away from God in self-disgust, and we feel hopeless because we have cut ourselves off from our only hope. Shame condemns us to sin again!

EXPLORE:
Jesus, have I been walking in a spirit of shame?

SOURCE:
If the source of shame has already been addressed and forgiven, then skip this. If not, ask: *What is the source of my shame?*

As necessary: Repent for sin. Receive forgiveness. Forgive others for sins and wounds against us.

Repent for our sinful reactions to them.

LIE: Perhaps: *Jesus, is there a lie attached to my shame?* If so, Renounce the lie. Receive truth from Him in exchange. Rejoice!

THANK JESUS: *I thank You Jesus that You were despised on my behalf, that You bore my sin as well as my grief and sorrow over it* (Isaiah 53:3-5). *Thank You for bearing my shame so I can be free of it!*

REPENT: *Jesus, I repent for embracing shame instead of bringing it to You.* Place the weight of pain, sin and shame on Jesus' body on the cross.

BREAK OFF: *By the authority of Christ, I bind the spirit of shame and send it to Jesus' feet.*

EXCHANGE: *Jesus, what do You have for me in exchange for shame?* Rejoice!

CHAPTER 16

Tending Your Heart

*T*he goal of this book has been to facilitate intimacy with God by offering ways to invite Him into our everyday lives, overcome hindrances and experience more of His heart. Again, our desire is not to promote any techniques or methods that we rigidly adhere to, but to offer handrails to launch us into a deeper and more enjoyable friendship with our Father.

Tending Your Heart is a simple tool to cultivate abiding in Jesus. As you capture the essence of it, you will find the help we have given in this book can be drawn upon to enrich your relationship with Him. More than any other material we offer, *Tending Your Heart*, which we will walk you through in this chapter, is being used by the Lord to transform lives. Even mature believers are finding their relationship with Him revitalized.

True Discipleship

In our church, and the dozens of churches that have been planted from it, discipleship is recognized as a critical component in our life together with Jesus. We are so grateful for this emphasis because discipleship is sorely neglected in much of the body of Christ. It is wonderful to have community, brothers and sisters in Christ to walk with, to have an environment of encouragement, to be affirmed and helped, to have those committed to our welfare who will, in love, hold us accountable. In fact, many can attest to the fact that without brothers and sisters to walk with, without mentors and role models, they very much doubt if they would have overcome their challenges and grown in their relationship with Jesus.

But, we have to ask these questions: *What happens when we do not have a supportive community of believers? What happens if we are in a church that is unhealthy, or we have no access to any genuine fellowship around Jesus? What happens when our family doesn't want to have anything to do with God? What happens when we are isolated and alone, working for a boss who constantly demeans us? What happens when we have no support or encouragement?*

> *Our need as believers is to become, primarily, disciples of Jesus Himself and not any other role model, no matter how gifted or helpful they may be.*

True discipleship is teaching and modeling how to process and receive directly from Jesus as source. Only then can we thrive in our relationship with Him regardless of circumstances.

Even if we are blessed to have rich fellowship, we are never encouraged in Scripture to depend upon or put our hope in one another. Our hope must be in Jesus alone. The body of Christ is filled with those who have put their hope in fellow believers only to have those hopes shattered, and with it, all too often, their confidence in God Himself.

Having said that, he who deliberately isolates himself from the body is rejecting Christ Himself who lives in His saints! True, we are all in process and can hurt one another, but our Father is absolutely committed to us as His children, and He commands us to preserve the unity of the Spirit (Ephesians 2:3), the common life of Jesus we all share. The New Testament is full of one another's–being knit together, fitly joined, honoring, loving, serving one another–for no member of the body can say to another, "I have no need of you" (1 Corinthians 12:21). There is a unique expression of Christ in every believer that is priceless, and from which we can all learn.

Unfortunately, especially among this generation of believers, dependence upon other Jesus followers, whether leaders or peers, far too often outweighs dependence upon Christ.

I (Rick) have had guys struggling with some issue come to me and say along these lines: *Well, I didn't have any mentor or discipler. I had no one to help me, so of course I'm going to get stuck.* They have not discovered the riches they have access to in Christ Himself. An effective discipler must simply model and show the disciple how to connect with Jesus and get what their heart needs from Him. This can begin the very day they come to Christ.

A college girl, who had no understanding of life as a Christian, was led to Christ by her fellow students. Immediately, they encouraged her to ask Jesus what He had to say to her. She responded that she didn't get any words but a picture. She said she was sitting on her front porch early in the morning with a cup of coffee and seated next to her was Jesus and they were chatting together. The students were ecstatic that this girl was receiving, directly from Jesus, encouragement to spend time with Him first thing in her day, before they had a chance to give her input. She would never forget this.

Josef, a young Moslem in North Africa, was led to give his life to Jesus by a college student visiting his country. Immediately, Josef was encouraged to ask Jesus, *How do You see me?* After a pause, Josef replied that he didn't hear anything, but he did receive a picture. He said he saw a man dressed in a white robe holding a new-born baby. So, the student told Josef to ask Jesus what the picture meant. Jesus said: *I am the man and you are the baby. I'm holding you and you need to grow.* So, the new birth was revealed to Josef directly from Jesus!

As a discipler, you don't have to have all the answers. You don't have to be crushed by the emotional load of those you are discipling. True, as we have mentioned previously, we are to "bear one another's burdens" (Galatians 6:2), but we are to cast them onto Christ (1 Peter 1:7) who bears them for us.

The *Essence of Discipleship* article addresses this topic in a little more detail and is found in Resources (p.243).

This is what *Tending Your Heart* is all about–giving Jesus the opportunity to speak into our lives and disciple us Himself.

The Impact of Tending Your Heart

The enemy knows his time is short. We are bombarded with temptations and lies. The reports and survey results are now overwhelming. Many believers are struggling with their value and clarity of purpose, dealing with conflict in relation-ships, battling addictions and hidden sin.

If we learn to tend our hearts and stay connected with Jesus, we will be able to thrive in our relationship with Him no matter what is going on around us. Doing the one thing necessary–living by what He says to us.

A friend who was a doctor and worship leader, peacefully passed away in his sleep several years ago at the age of 50. He had this to say:

Connecting to the Father and 'tending my heart' has been the greatest gift since salvation. Because of it, I had freedoms I never thought possible. An enormous weight has been lifted.

Shackles have been removed. Sins no longer tempt me that I had problems with for decades. I can now breathe deeply with joy in my heart and I now know with confidence that Father loves me, Jesus is for me and will lead me every step of the way, and the Holy Spirit loves me and is there to support me every moment of my life. I now believe in my heart that I can truly do all things through Christ who strengthens me!

In our church planting school, leadership do not want anyone going into the field without knowing how to take care of their hearts by bringing them to Jesus. They have seen missionaries who have returned wounded, burned out, disillusioned and discouraged because they had not learned how to process with Jesus the pressures and difficulties they encountered.

Samuel, a church planter in North Africa, shared this:

I was first introduced to Tending Your Heart eight years ago when I was in a faith-based program for those recovering from substance abuse. I began going to the Father and asking Him what was wrong and why I had offense or why I was angry, and it really helped me through that process of coming out of addiction and into freedom. But, I didn't stop using it then. I still use it every day, years later. As a result, I have seen my relationship with the Father grow so much and so quickly. I am constantly talking with the Father, asking Him questions and getting His input and advice because who knows better than He does. He can see everything.

I've also seen a lot of growth in other people as I encourage friends, family members or people I encounter here in North Africa to go directly to the Father and ask Him to help them through situations or ask Him for clarity as to what is going on in their life. I have seen a lot of people grow really strong in their relationship with the Father and become dependent upon Him and less dependent upon other people. It is a beautiful thing because, as you are going through life, if you constantly have everyone coming to you with their problems, not only are you going to get tired, but you are going to become the person they look to instead of God, and that's not right.

> *Personally, I try to go to the Father first and take things to Him and I get His insight, His input and His help and wisdom.*

Then, if necessary, I take that 'information to the person who is my spiritual covering to make sure I'm on track. When we come to the Father first, it pleases Him. It makes Him happy because He created us and loves us, and He wants that close connection. I would encourage anyone who has access to Tending Your Heart to dig in and find out for yourself what it means to hear the Father's voice, to ask Him those deep things and get His insight into different areas of your life and you will be surprised how quickly and strongly you will grow in your relationship with Him.

Tending Your Heart is essentially a very simple tool that a new believer can easily grasp. It's an effective way to deal with hindrances to intimacy and begin to cultivate a lifestyle of two-way conversation with God.

The complete *Tending Your Heart* document without commentary is at the end of this chapter.

Follow along as we walk you through *Tending Your Heart* which is highlighted in bold and followed by commentary.

don't need to eat. Perhaps we'll gravitate to social media because we're feeling lonely. We'll turn to websites that will ensnare us. Maybe we'll simply bury ourselves in work and stay busy. We will go places we shouldn't go because we don't first turn to Jesus.

> *It takes no time to turn. He will never put us on hold, nor is He distracted. He's always ready and waiting. As soon as we turn, He is immediately and fully engaged. He died for this!*

Jesus: "Do not let your heart be troubled" ['agitated'] (John 14:1). We can choose! (Psalm 27:3)

Jesus is commanding us to not allow our hearts to be 'agitated' (AMP). *But,* we may counter, *life can be painfully difficult. I lost my job today and my car was just rear-ended.* Jesus wouldn't say that if we had no choice. He's saying that we are not victims. We have the power of the Holy Spirit, so we are always able to choose. Don't give fear any space. We can say *no.* In his Psalm (27:3), David simply says: "I *will not* fear." He may well have had good reason to fear, for an army was out to kill him, but still he chose not to.

Okay, so we have a choice, but how can we say no to anxiety when troubles threaten? We cannot avoid letting our hearts be agitated when troubles come, unless we are confident that Jesus can be trusted to overcome absolutely everything for us. That's exactly where proactively receiving His heart for us will give us growing confidence in His care.

Martin Luther said something like this:

> *You can't stop birds (demonic thoughts)*
> *from flying around your head, but there is no*
> *excuse for allowing them to nest in your hair.*

Don't let negative thoughts settle. Don't accommodate them. If we do give them permission, the enemy will ensure that others will follow. James 4:7 says that we are to actively resist the devil and he will flee. If the thought comes: *It's going to be a terrible day,* and I let it sit there, I will anticipate negative outcomes. So, when they arrive: *Bummer. Just as I thought.* If we are passive and don't reject that negative or unclean thought, the enemy will be sure to take advantage: *Well, he didn't toss that one off, so here's another, and another... This guy's a sitting duck for punishment.*

If it's not life-giving and helpful, it's not the Holy Spirit, so don't give that thought any room to land. Never enter into conversation with the enemy by asking: *What makes you so sure it's going to be a terrible day?* He would love to convince you. Instead, you can say: *I don't receive that. I reject that thought. Father, what do You have to say?* He may say, *I'm so glad you asked me. Stick with Me, and it'll be an amazing day! Let Me tell you how you can do that.*

Imagine the freedom if we did not receive any negative thought?

A young lady who suffered from severe, debilitating depression wrote Diane: *I would cycle out of deep, deep depression every few days. There hasn't been a trace of depression in me. None! (after 7 months). My life is totally different now as I see myself as a daughter of God the Father. Tending Your Heart has been the key to it all.* She learned to receive her true identity from the Father and His love for her, so she was able to recognize and reject those negative thoughts, turn to the Father and hear again and again His words that met her heart.

The more we taste the reality and truth of God's words, the more quickly we recognize the counterfeit and are able to nip those negative thoughts in the bud before they take root.

2. **ASK: When moved away from security and rest, turn your mind and heart to God and ask (aloud if possible):**
    - *Father what is this really about?* **(Psalm 139:23, 24)**
    - **Listen and don't discount what you receive.**
    - **He may reveal: sin you need to repent of, a lie you believe, someone you need to forgive, a spirit you have given access to, etc.**

It's good to ask God a question aloud if we can. It helps our hearts get into a receptive posture where we are more expectant.

Recognizing the Father knows us so much better than we do, we ask Him why we are triggered. We don't need to try and figure it out. At best, we are guessing anyway. We may get it right, but we can never be sure. King David asked the Father to search his heart and lead him (Psalm 139:23, 24). He didn't introspect and try to diagnose himself. The apostle Paul said: *"I do not even examine myself ... the one who examines me is the Lord"* (1 Corinthians 4:3, 4).

> *We can spend hours trying to figure what's going on in our hearts, but God can put His finger on the core issue in a moment.*

We tend to discount our first impression after we ask God a question, thinking it's just us. Too often we blow it off and then complain God never speaks to us. Of course, there is no guarantee that the first impression is from Him, but it is stunning how often it is because He is often so eager to speak to us. For many of us, He has been waiting a very long time for us, not only to ask Him a question, but for us to wait for His answer.

3. **RECOGNIZE honestly and humbly admit any lie or action you need to take and follow His lead. Forgive and bless others where necessary.**

If Jesus reveals we have been believing a lie and need to forgive someone who led us to believe it, make sure you ask Him what the heart wound is that you need to forgive for.

4. **RENOUNCE the lie (aloud if possible) and break off any partnership with the enemy.**

Remember that when we believe a lie we are rejecting the Holy Spirit of truth and agreeing with the enemy.

5. **REPENT for partnering with the enemy and giving the lie authority. Ask forgiveness for any sin God reveals or any sinful reaction to your wound by self-protection, denial, self-comfort, etc.**

Let's step back and take a broad look at what we are doing here when we are triggered. Once we are triggered, we bring it to God, ask Him about it and respond to Him. We are simply cooperating with God to address flesh patterns and reactions that block our hearts and prevent us from what is

most critical–receiving what God h the word of Christ." The
heart space for Him.   l, spoken word; the living
    In the parable of the sower (Luk ible, the logos, but it's the
four kinds of hearts and their recep word that throbs with life
of God. If we continue to believe lie ring" in this verse, means
we harbor unforgiveness, if we refu art. Receiving these living
our sin, then the hardened soil of o arts, all the accusations,
fully receive His life-giving seed. W ny. Beyond that, God will
but the life in it will be hindered ur day and fill me with joy and
with any heart blockages. For His
penetrate the soil, the heart must b e spirit" (Ephesians 6:17),
from rocks and weeds and other lo the rhema word. Our con-
do what the Sower intended – to p s lies comes as the Spirit
    Remember, the word must pe n 5:7) that this word is for
accomplish its purpose, for it is wit
The whole point of tending our he we are familiar with the
triggered, is to take care of anyth irit is able to bring them to
that we can truly receive at a hear our hearts. The Scriptures
So, when He tells me He is delig ur heads and go no deeper
without hesitation: *Yes! Thank Yo* re inspired, God-breathed,
I hope so.   which He desires to com-
    As we have noted, we are to li
(Matthew 4:4). Moreover, we are that the enemy is always
1:17), and faith comes by hearing cy with God. Ha! The orig-
10:17). Because it is with the hea renounced lies and closed
10:10), then receiving His word ir to receive the truth into our
is to transform us. And, make no re believed there.
will determine our actions.   ith temptations, lies and sin
                                 ou have not been receiving
                                 you.

———————✳—

> *If we fill our hearts with what He speaks to us,*
> *the enemy will have difficulty getting*
> *his foot in the door*

– although he sure will try banging on it!

If I only receive the truth at a cerebral level and mentally assent to it, it won't help me very much. Psalm 51:6 says, "You desire truth in the innermost being." Information in our minds will not be enough to resist temptation. I meet guys all the time who know some applicable scriptures but struggle with pornography. The scribes of Jesus' day knew the scriptures backwards, but they crucified Jesus. Why? Because their hearts were empty. Psalm 119:11 says, "Your word have I hid in my heart that I may not sin against You." His truth must penetrate our hearts to bring transformation – and if we receive it, it will, without a doubt, bring life change.

Remember that Mary, Martha and Lazarus' sister, who we read of in Luke 10:39, knew how to receive what Jesus said because, as noted in Romans 10:10, what we receive and embrace in the heart is what we believe. And what we truly believe will be expressed in our lives. It was Mary who, later, in an act of profound worship, ministered to Jesus, anointing Him with very costly perfume (John 12:3).

The word 'know' (Gk. *ginosko*) as used so often by John in his letters ("we have come to know and believe the love which God has for us" – 1 John 4:16), does not mean intellectual assent. It more accurately means *experiential knowledge* through the work of the Holy Spirit. It is knowledge that pierces our hearts so that we can be certain, without doubt. We may not be able to articulate it or explain it, but we have a heartfelt assurance that what God is saying to us is true.

To sum up then, any lies we have believed, we have believed with our hearts, so once we have renounced a lie we must replace it with truth – in our hearts. That's why we always should ask the Father what He has for our hearts in exchange for whatever has been blocking our intimacy with Him.

We encourage you to journal what the Father gives you. It may be encouraging words, a scripture or a picture that you may ask Him about. We call it a *Listening Journal*. It amazes me to see how well the Father reads my mail and how eager He is to give me insight and help just where I need it. Often, He will ask me to go back and reread what He has been saying to me, and I always find huge encouragement there, frequently with more impact than when He first spoke it.

So, how can we partner with the Holy Spirit so that the words He speaks are able to penetrate deeper than our understanding and become reality in our hearts?

7. **REJOICE in what God has given you in exchange for the lie (aloud if possible)! Declare it over your life. Thank Him and worship. Ask for more. Unpack it with Him until practical and helpful.**

Few believers seem to recognize the importance of rejoicing and declaring aloud what God speaks so that our hearts are able to fully receive the life and power in His words and what He says doesn't just remain mental assent. If the Father simply says to me, *Rick, I love you!* and my response is, *Okay, that's nice. I have known that for a while. Is that all?* Then I've missed it.

But, what a world of difference if I take hold of those words and declare:

Father, thank You that You love me!

Thank You that You know me through and through and yet love me just the way I am!

213

Thank You that I don't have to change for You to love me any more than You do! Thank You that I can depend on your love for me no matter what I think or feel! Thank You that even when I blow it You stay committed to me, that You have the very best for me!

As I hear my own voice declaring the truth that the Father has spoken to me, my heart begins to rejoice. The Holy Spirit within bears witness to the truth and leaps for joy. This is an effective way of tapping into the river of life and refreshment we have within that Jesus promised (John 7:38).

Receiving the words of the Father into our hearts is vividly illustrated by Jeremiah (15:16). "Your words were found, and I ate them, and your words became for me a joy and the delight of my heart." As we slow down, meditate on and digest His words of life that we are created to live by, we experience their reality and our hearts are filled.

It is necessary to not only hear from God but learn to receive what He says in our hearts if we are to thrive in our life with Him.

DON'T LEAVE HUNGRY

How it must grieve the Father that far too often we come to Him with little expectation that we are going to get much help.

> *It's like He has a huge banquet table laden with delicious and nutritious food, but we walk away with a few nacho chips thinking, Well, that was kind of lame.*

We read the words about abundant life or "the riches of His grace which He lavished upon us" (Ephesians 1:7,8) but we

the Father about it, it su̶out – burdened with a mind-
nothing more than to see̶nds were largely oblivious to.
Also, I encourage you̶e away. He was attractive to
̶t rest that He had plenty to
*unpack wh̶*u who are weary and heavy
practic̶(Matthew 11:28). He was so
̶e crowds, "He who comes to
*Jesus, thank You for You̶*5). He lived so refreshed that
*in this particular situation̶*rsty, let Him come to Me and
that I can stay in peace?
*love but how can I love m̶*Jesus, fully man, "tempted in
her heart in this season?"̶ut sin" (Hebrews 4:15)? He
̶eeded from His Father. I am
JESUS, OUR MODEL
̶is baptism: "My beloved Son
̶Luke 3:22) that it wasn't the
Perhaps we find ourse̶lis true Father (Luke 2:49). In
by pressures. Don't forget̶e demands and accusations,
̶ellowship, understanding and
*no one has̶*often retreat from the crowds
*pressu̶*Luke 5:16). I can imagine: *Son,*
̶*are loving him so well.*

He had only three and a h̶
ciples did not act like the s̶
they were going to be critic̶n *utterly depleted in no*
church. He knew that cruci̶*ed how to receive from*
was impatient or frustrated̶*'s heart needed.*
were slow to learn, that H̶
necessary for the salvation̶thing without His Father (John
He could see men's he̶us how we too can live in con-
brokenness around Him. N̶ He did. How is that possible?
continually. Knowing what ̶led, equipped and sustained
Him to be so focused, batt̶ Him, all we need to thrive; the
tions of the enemy throwing̶ck of the enemy; the power to
totally understand if Jesu̶life, to enjoy unbroken intimacy

with the Father; to receive His rest and His joy, and to fulfill our destiny.

PERSISTENT BURDEN OR PAIN

We addressed Processing Grief and Loss in detail in Chapter 10 but in *Tending Your Heart* there is a note in Step 2:

If there is a heavy or persistent burden, pain or grief, then see note below ***
   This brief footnote is a summary, giving some basic steps to process with Jesus in these areas.

*** Pour out your heart to Him (Psalm 62:8).
   Be encouraged by David's honesty. God is not shockable. Tell Him how you feel.

Cast your care onto Him (1Peter 5:7).
   To cast means to throw down. Don't just bring your cares to Him and then walk away still holding onto them. Let them go. Give them to Him. Only when your "hands" are empty are they in a position to receive from Him.

Place it on His body on the cross (Isaiah 53:4a).
   What incredible pain Jesus must have carried on the cross! This passage said that He bore the world's pain and sorrow! Surely, He died of a broken heart! If we give our burden to Him, trust Him to bear it for us, only then are our hearts free to receive all He has to pour into us.

Let Him comfort you (2 Corinthians 1:3,4).
   Because Jesus knows the depth of our pain like no one else, He knows exactly how to meet us there. More than that,

He died to make that comfort available. He is that motivated to help us!

Receive His exchange (Isaiah 61:1-3).

My experience is, that no matter what we surrender to Him and trust Him with, He always proves Himself faithful and blows us away with His kindness. I give Him the things that weigh me down or trouble me, and He gives me His peace and rest which increases as I rejoice in what He pours into my heart. He always trades up! In fact, in retrospect, I always wish I had been quicker to trust Him more.

GROWING INTO WHAT YOU HAVE RECEIVED

To consolidate and continue to grow in your freedom in Christ, it is very helpful to revisit the exchanges He has given you, regularly declaring and rejoicing over them. Find Scriptures that articulate His exchanges. List them and declare them until you find you are easily living in their reality. You will find this life-giving, transformative and fun! And, yes, it can be a springboard to further exchanges.

You will find a useful summary, *Tending Your Heart - Overview*, in Resources (p.246)

JOURNAL TENDING YOUR HEART

"We are destroying speculations and every lofty thing raised up against the knowledge of God and we are taking every thought captive to the obedience of Christ" (2 Corinthians 10:5).

<u>Suggested questions</u>:

Father, what area in my life right now do I need to ask You about?
> Relationship with God, others?
> Difficult circumstances, family pressures, etc.?
> *What revelation do You have for me about this?*
> *How do You want me to cooperate with You here?*

Father, in what area of my life am I most prone to think negatively or be discouraged?
> *What do I believe that causes this?*
> *What do You have to say about that?*
> *How do You want me to tend my heart more effectively in this area?*

Father, what does my heart need to hear from You right now?
> *Do I find it difficult to receive this from You in a way that makes a difference?*
> *What do I need to do to position my heart to receive more deeply?*

is eager to capture and transform us into His likeness as He speaks to our hearts.

Diane

When the Holy Spirit takes the words He has written and highlights them on the page, bringing them to life for us personally, we are able to get far more meaning if we unpack those words in conversation with God. They become more life-giving for us. We do this simply by asking Him questions about any scripture that resonates with us or captures our attention. As I have done this, I have gained more revelation out of the written word than I have ever received before which has brought greater freedom and transformation.

In this way, we experience the combined power of the written word of God (logos) and the spoken, personalized word of God (rhema). Through His rhema we gain a fuller understanding of the heart of God as revealed in Scripture and, in my experience, often more powerfully than in any other way.

We can unpack these highlighted scriptures further by asking questions of Him until what we receive is practical and encouraging, so that we can understand how to cooperate with Him and obey Him so that the power of His love is released in and through us.

This is not reading Scripture to study, to gain a limited, rational understanding, as valuable as that may be.

> *This is entering into conversation directly with the author of the Bible Himself and allowing the Holy Spirit to take us deeper into the living truth behind the words on the page.*

When the Holy Spirit highlights a truth in your spirit, stop and unpack it with Him. Turn it into conversation with Him, asking Him about it. *What does this mean? How do I cooperate with You to walk this out?* Write down the flow of what He gives you. Your Bible study will be hugely magnified and enlivened!

A few years ago, I was living in constant pain originating 35 years earlier when thrown from a horse on my honeymoon in Tasmania, so I had to have a hip replacement. I was overwhelmed at what lay before us. It was at a time when our church's discipleship and church-planting schools were starting back up and college students were returning for their school year and our involvement would be the most intense. I thought: *There is no way I can do this!*

One day I was reading Isaiah 66:13: "As one whom His mother comforts, so I will comfort you." All of a sudden, great emotion welled up in me and I recognized this was the Holy Spirit highlighting this verse for me.

And so, I asked Him: *What is this? What is triggering me? Where do I most need comfort from You?*

And He said: *In the places of your weakness and doubt, where you feel vulnerable and overwhelmed.*

How do I receive that comfort?

You must come to Me for it. Give Me all your care, fear, weakness and fragility. I want to carry you and meet you in every area of your fear. Fear separates us because you retreat into avoidance, seeking to submerge your fear into meaningless activity and occupy your mind with things. You must face your fears with Me and let Me take them and deliver you from the snare of the enemy.

As we praise Him with thanksgiving for what He has spoken to us, we can receive the life of His words into our

hearts that builds our faith, reinforces our true identity, re
our mind, and brings transformation and freedom.

We may be used to reading Scripture quickly and of ﹍﹍
shallowly, but this is where we take a very small portion that
has stood out to us, enter into conversation with God about
it, and journal what He says.

The examples that follow are personal to me. As God
speaks to each of us in this way, it will be unique and fit our
personality. Remember, we can test what we receive for it
must line up with Scripture and with His character.

Here is an excerpt from my journal in June 2012, in a
season when I needed refreshment.
I read, "Ask and it will be given. Seek and you will find"
(Matthew 7:7).
I said: *Lord, I ask for refreshment and rest. How do I seek it?
Seek Me. Life and rest are in Me. Refreshment is in Me.*
I went on to unpack it with Him to make it practical and doable
in my life day-to-day.

In July 2014, I was meditating on rest, asking Him each
day what rest looks like. Psalm 107:9 really resonated with
me. "He satisfies the longing soul and fills the hungry with
goodness."
I asked: *How do You want to satisfy me Lord?*
*I long to give you all you need, to fill your heart and life to
overflowing. There is no lack in My presence. And all the
fragile weak places I want to turn into places of sweet rest.
Lord, how do I open myself to this more fully?
Surrender. Don't strive or seek to experience something. Just
surrender to the sweetness of my presence. Let it wash over
you. You are weary, and I want to give you rest.*

Here is another example of entering into conversation
with God over a Scripture that brought greater revelation.
1 Peter 4:14 "… the spirit of glory and of God rests on you."

227

Whoa! I was so struck by this and felt to ask, *Lord is it Your splendor upon me that You see?*
When I look at you, I see My finished work. I rejoice and delight in all that I will have in you for all eternity. We will have the ages to share in that beauty and oneness. You have so many things you look at when you are thinking of yourself. You see the holes, the incompleteness, the flaws, the darkness. I don't see the shadows. I see the glory. Because you see My glory is truly upon you and it has overcome everything else. Just look at My glory and everything else will fade away. It will draw you out to run with who you really are. Share My joy over you and let me bring you fully into the light of My love."

I want to end with this thought from Jeremiah 9:23,24. "'Let not the wise man boast in his wisdom, the mighty man in his might, or the rich man in his riches. But let him who boasts, boast in this, that he understands and knows Me, that I am the Lord who exercises lovingkindness, justice and righteousness on earth; for I delight in these things,' declares the Lord."

Rick

It is clear, simply from the Scriptures themselves, that God wants to speak to us personally about them. After all, they are inspired or "God-breathed" (2 Timothy 3:16). Jesus said: "The words I speak to you are spirit and life" (John 6:63). He wants His words to do more than convey information to our minds, but to come to life for us – to reach our hearts and transform us.

Numerous times He mentions both the written law and His speaking in the same context. "And the Lord said: 'Because they have forsaken My law which I set before them and have not obeyed My voice nor walked according to it ..."" (Jeremiah 9:13).

Referencing Deuteronomy 8:3, Jesus rebuked Satan with "Man shall not live on bread alone but on every word (personal, spoken 'rhema') that proceeds out of the mouth of God" (Matthew 4:4). As we mentioned earlier, Jesus modeled the lifestyle He invites us into, living His life on earth in response to what He saw the Father doing and what He heard the Father saying. But, notice the context. Jesus rebuked the enemy's temptation by quoting Scripture: "It is written ..." In fact, each of the three temptations in the wilderness, Jesus repulsed by quoting Scripture. What significance is there for us here?

Jesus spoke by responding to the rhema word of His Father. This means that the scriptures He used in this encounter were highlighted to Jesus by His Father! Jesus was not just using His knowledge of Scripture to counter a challenge. He defeated the enemy by declaring what the Father spoke to Him from the Scripture. Here we see the intended power of the logos when it is brought to life through the rhema!

The foundation and object of faith

I have often heard it said, *I am believing God for this.* It could be that we want something very badly or maybe we are convinced that this is something God wants. For me, it begs the question: *What is the source of our confidence in a specific outcome?*

"Faith comes by hearing and hearing by the word (*rhema* – the personal, spoken word) of Christ" (Romans 10:17). We cannot claim a scripture we find that fits our situation as though we have God over a barrel, and then insist that He come through in the way we expect because we have got it from Him in black and white.

In the wilderness, the devil took scriptures (Psalm 91:11,12) and goaded Jesus to jump down from the pinnacle of the temple, saying: "It is written, [just as Jesus did!] 'He will give His angels charge concerning You' and 'On their hands they will bear You up, lest You strike Your foot against a stone'" (Matthew 4:6).

> *If we claim scriptures without listening to the Author, we can risk presumption.*

When I was young, it was called, *Name it and Claim it.* Many were deeply disillusioned, and all too often God was dishonored.

Now, of course, the Bible is full of encouragement for us to be confident in the power and kindness of God. By all means, we can take those verses and rejoice that in a specific situation He will prove Himself faithful as we trust Him. But we cannot claim a specific outcome unless God has clearly spoken or highlighted it to us by His Spirit. That kind of faith "comes by hearing."

As mentioned earlier, "Hearing" in Romans 10:17 means receiving into the heart so as to believe. And if we truly believe, our actions will reveal it. Paul asks: "Does He, then, who provides you with the Spirit and work miracles among you, do it by the works of the law or by hearing with faith?" (Galatians 3:5). So, then, receiving the Spirit and having miracles worked through us are simply the result of taking to heart what God says – and obeying.

Nevertheless, to take this further, even if we are convinced God has given us a promise for a specific situation, we can easily be inclined to think that we must hold onto that promise for God to follow through and fulfill it. All too often, we take upon ourselves the pressure to be faithful and so we are unable to inwardly rest. It's easy to feel it depends upon us and not upon the faithfulness of God. As exemplified by "the father of our faith," Abraham, we must surrender back to God our Isaacs, even the promise He has clearly given, if we are to experience His peace and comfort in the midst of trials. Without surrender, letting go and giving back to God those promises we sense He has given us and entrusting Him with them, we are not able to receive the grace He has for us in the present.

The surrender of our hearts and desires to God is the ultimate act of faith. I am not talking about resignation, which doubts His goodness, but trusting God to take our burden or the promises or gifts He has given us and handle them kindly and faithfully. It also means trusting Him to help us to be faithful and responsive to His leading. To cling to a promise out of fear that it depends upon me alone to carry the burden faithfully is not trusting Him.

Here is a tension. Yes, we are encouraged to persevere in prayer. And yes, we are encouraged to ask and keep on asking, the literal meaning of Matthew 7:7. But, we are also encouraged to trust in the goodness and sovereignty of God.

> We must hold fast to the heart of God and the kindness of His ways and hold lightly the specific outcome we desire.

Recently, a father who had lost his 4-month-old daughter to SIDS, said at her memorial service that it is not the degree or quality of our faith that matters but the object of our faith, Jesus Christ Himself. The foundation for our faith must be the faithfulness and goodness of God Himself, regardless of

es or outcomes. That kind of confidence in Him
we learn to surrender our desires to Him, again
, and position ourselves to receive His abundant
jement, comfort and peace.

Invitation to friendship, not formulas and my Dad's healing

As a 19-year-old, I became excited about what the Scripture had to say about Jesus' desire to heal – today. I began to imagine all the ways a supernatural healing would cause unbelievers to stop and pay attention to the claims of Christ. This had incredible implications!

As I poured over all the healing scriptures, my analytical mind kicked in. According to the gospels, everyone who came to Jesus for healing, received it. He never turned anyone away. Nor did He ever tell them to wait. Then, there is the verse, "Jesus Christ is the same yesterday and today and forever" (Hebrews 13:8). Therefore, I reasoned, because Jesus lives in me by His Holy Spirit, then He wants to heal the sick through me. I just have to believe Him, and He will do it. 1+1=2. Simple. How had we missed it? Wow!

Now in those days, the late 60's, in Australia, the idea that Jesus still heals today was radical for most believers. For years, my Dad suffered terribly from migraines and so I approached him one Sunday afternoon, Bible in hand, when he was lying on his bed writhing in pain. He was a wonderful, godly man but I was not sure where he stood on the matter of healing. So, after sharing some scriptures, I asked him if he had asked Jesus to heal him. He told me that of course he had prayed. Then, he invited me to pray for him. Suddenly, I felt pressure. Would I have the faith to see a miracle?

I poured out my heart to God and asked for healing, quoting scriptures I had underlined in my Bible. When I

ADDENDUM

Praying from the throne or from under the pile?

How can we pray and intercede for desperate needs without being crushed by them?

For a few years now, the Father has been encouraging me (Rick) to rejoice in the face of difficulties and trials. Frankly, I sometimes find it a bit of a stretch when James exhorts us to "Count it all joy my brothers, when you encounter various trials" (James 1:2). But there's a priceless secret here! All too often, in a difficult situation, I used to pray something like this: *Oh Lord, can You please help me? Can You somehow work in this?*

The Holy Spirit alerted me that when I pray this way I can easily be praying from a place of unbelief. It's as if I am pleading with God because I am not so sure He will actually help me or those I pray for. Perhaps because of my own weakness, He will withhold His intervention, maybe to teach me something. If I am not convinced of His willingness to help me, I may feel that I need to convince Him, to motivate Him. So, my request is built on a false assumption about the heart of God towards me or for those I intercede for.

The Holy Spirit encourages us to come to God confident that He will reward us. "…he who comes to God must believe that He is, and that He is a rewarder of those who seek Him" arted!

Hebrews 11:6). Jesus goes further: "He who comes to Me will not hunger and he who believes in Me will never thirst" (John 6:35). "Let us therefore draw near with confidence to the throne of grace that we may receive mercy and may find grace to help in time of need" (Hebrews 4:16).

Here is a simple key that I have found has often produced a vital switch in the way I pray about a need or a burden. Let me first say, that I am not necessarily talking about severe grief and loss, which we discussed in Chapter 10. As I present the difficulty to God, I usually *begin by thanking Him for who He is*, declaring His kindness and faithfulness. As David understood: "You are enthroned on the praises of Israel" (Psalm 22:3). Immediately, some may protest. *How can I worship when I have this issue weighing down on me?*

In our spirits, true to our new nature, we want to praise and thank God no matter what circumstances are threatening to crush us or are causing our feelings to scream. As someone said, *Don't put your emotions in the trunk, but they can't drive the car either.* Our spirits need to lead our souls - our thoughts feelings and decisions. We can activate and strengthen our spirits by worship and thanksgiving. Doing it aloud is far more effective. So, in fact, thanking the Father for His faithfulness and kindness, is exactly what our souls need to hear so our thoughts and emotions can be renewed and we are able to receive His peace, even in the midst of trials.

As I praise Him, the Spirit within me bears witness and my confidence grows that God is so much bigger than the problem I am concerned about which enables me to pray with expectancy in His intervention. My Father is on His throne and as I exalt Him, the unstoppable power of His love is unleashed.

> *Once the eyes of my heart are fixed on the faithful heart of God, then I am able to bring Him the need, not begging and pleading, but rather rejoicing*

that He knows the need much more than I, that He is far more motivated to bring redemption into that situation, and that as I pray, I can rejoice that He hears the cry of my heart and that I can trust His Spirit to immediately address it.

Back in the 1980s in Tasmania, I still vividly recall gathering with a bunch of new believers for a time of prayer. Even though there were many needs and concerns in the room—struggles with temptations, financial and relational issues, and so on—we simply and spontaneously began to worship. As we did, the Holy Spirit added more content to our worship. We praised the Father for His patience, His readiness to forgive, His relentless pursuit, the power of His Spirit within us, the joy of being in His family, under His covering and care. The atmosphere was electric as the power of His love filled our hearts. The time flew by and then we realized we had not started praying specifically for the needs. But then, as we called out our burdens, we found even more reason to thank God and worship as we were given the absolute assurance and comfort that He was already faithfully taking care of our concerns.

Even though Habakkuk's crops failed, and his cattle stalls were empty, he declared, *yet I will exult in the Lord, I will rejoice in the God of my salvation* (3:17-19). And of course, Paul, a seasoned warrior in the spiritual realm is emphatic: *Rejoice in the Lord always; again, I will say, rejoice!* (Philippians 4:4). We cannot often be sure of a specific outcome, but we can always confidently anticipate and rejoice in the goodness of God at work in the needs we bring to Him.

As we rejoice in the Lord in the face of adversity or spiritual dryness, it makes a way in our hearts for Him to meet us there. "Sing to the Lord, sing praises to His name; Cast up a highway for Him who rides through the deserts" (Psalm 68:4).

It is amazing how different perspectives on a challenging situation can have a dramatic impact on how we respond. One can be crippled by disappointment, bitterness or confusion, while another, facing the same circumstance, can be drawn to a deeper appreciation of the Lord's sovereign kindness. When we are faced with a challenge, if we first lift our hearts and voices in praise and thanksgiving for the love and power of our Father, our perspective is more easily aligned with His, and we are able to pray with authority and assurance, seated with Him in heavenly places (Ephesians 2:6) and not crushed under the pile of our own perceptions.

ASK HIM AND JOURNAL

Father, are there ways I have been praying to You that You want to talk with me about?

How do You want me to cooperate with You, so I can pray in a life-giving way that unleashes Your Spirit?

Father, what does it mean to You when I rejoice in You in the face of challenges?

RESOURCES

HEARING GOD AND EXPECTANCY

Take one or two of these scriptures.

Referring to different translations may be helpful.

Ask these questions directly to the Father or Jesus and journal what He says.

Matthew 27:50, 51 Access to Holy of Holies.

Exodus 25:22 "I will meet with you ... speak to you"

What are these scriptures saying about
1) Your desire? 3) My ability to hear You?

Psalm 95:7,8 "Today if you want to hear His voice, do not harden your hearts."
What ways do I harden my heart to hearing
You?

Jeremiah 33:3 "Call to Me and I will answer you and I will tell you great ... things which you do not know."
What rises up in me when I think about
dreaming with You?
What do You want me to say to encourage me
to dream with You?

Isaiah 58:9,11 "You will cry, and He will say, 'Here I am'…The Lord will guide you continually."
> *What have I believed about Your guidance in my life?*

Isaiah 30:21 "You will hear a word from your Teacher … whenever you turn"
> *If I believe this is true, how do You want me to respond?*

Isaiah 1:18 "Come now and let us reason together."
> *What stops me bringing my doubts, questions and concerns to You?*

John 10:27 "My sheep hear Me;" Jn.10:3 "He calls His own sheep by name."
> *What do I believe about being able to hear You?*

Isaiah 9:6 "Counselor;" Jn.20:17 "your Father;" Jn.15:14 "My friends" - Includes conversation
> *What has conversation with You looked like in my life?*
> *How do You want to encourage me here?*

Revelation 3:20 "If anyone hears My voice … opens the door I will come in … dine with him and he with Me."
> *How do You want me to open the door to You?*
> *How do You want me to share more of my heart with You?*

THE ESSENCE OF DISCIPLESHIP

Discipleship is making disciples of *Jesus*. Okay, that's obvious when we think about it, but helping people really connect with Jesus tends to be overshadowed by a list of tasks to be fulfilled: reading Scripture, praying to Jesus, pursuing fellowship and accountability, sharing our faith, and so on.

John, the baptizer, demonstrates this (John 1:36, 37). He first "looked upon Jesus as He walked" and then directed his listeners to "Behold the Lamb of God". (To behold is to look earnestly, with a view to learning.) Two of his disciples who heard Him speak, no longer followed John but "followed Jesus."

Jesus Himself modeled discipleship for us. He was discipled by His Father. "He awakens Me morning by morning. He awakens My ear to listen as a disciple" (Isaiah 50:4, 5). "I do nothing on My own initiative, but I speak these things as the Father taught Me" (John 8:28).

If we are to be discipled by Jesus, then our primary goal is to learn how to hear and respond to Him. Whether we are reading Scripture, walking with other believers or sharing our faith, we need to be open to the instruction of the Holy Spirit who has been given as our helper to lead us into all truth. Dependence on Him is even necessary if we are to pray effectively (Romans 8:26). And, of course, praying itself is severely limited and soon becomes robbed of enjoyment if we are not listening to Him so He can guide and encourage us.

Disciplers all too often find they are weighed down and drained by trying to give the disciples the answers and help they need. Now of course, patience and endurance are often required in coming alongside someone and helping them grow in Christ. The problem is that

> *disciplers often cultivate, maybe unwittingly,*
> *a dependence upon themselves as source—*
> *instead of dependence upon Jesus.*
> *What a relief it is for disciplers to recognize*
> *the radical difference!*

From the outset, a disciple should learn they can turn to Jesus, ask Him about anything and receive what He has for them. That they can bring to Him burdens and difficulties, problems and pain, and get help and encouragement directly from the one who knows and understands them like no other.

Disciplers are only effective to the degree that they point others to Jesus and help them engage with Him!

Sadly, it is all too common for disciples to become so dependent on the discipler, mentor, elder, pastor or close friend that they are at a loss when they find themselves in a situation where they no longer have access to their help and encouragement. They have not experienced the reality of deep friendship with Jesus. They have not cultivated a lifestyle of enjoyable intimacy with Him that will meet the deepest needs of their hearts.

Modeling and leading disciples to enter a simple two-way conversation with God builds confidence in turning to Him as their Father, Comforter, Shepherd, Teacher, Guide, Healer, Deliverer and closest Friend. Impediments to our growth in Christ will be revealed and overcome as we come to the "Wonderful Counselor" (Isaiah 9:6).

The disciple is not limited to the strengths or weaknesses of the discipler but is able to access the unlimited counsel of God!

This is why every discipler should learn how to facilitate the disciple's connection with Jesus.

Cultivating a lifestyle of *Tending Your Heart* is a simple and very effective way to facilitate dialogue with Jesus— enjoying His companionship, processing heart issues with Him and learning from Him.

Confidence in coming to Jesus and immediately receiving from Him what our hearts need is the birthright and gift offered every believer.

TENDING YOUR HEART - OVERVIEW

INTIMACY WITH GOD – OUR ABSOLUTE PRIORITY

Jesus died so we could enjoy intimacy with Him – dialogue, sharing hearts (Matthew 27:50.51; Exodus 25:22).

We are to live listening to Him (Deuteronomy 8:3; Matthew 4:4).

Jesus modeled this (John 5:19; 8:26,28).

Jesus said there is only one thing necessary (Luke 10:39).

We can all hear Him speak (John 10:27)

By cultivating a lifestyle of proactively listening to and receiving from God, we are able to enjoy increasing intimacy with Him and deny the enemy opportunity to rob us.

OVERCOMING HINDRANCES

The enemy's strategy is to prevent intimacy with God. Without it we are ineffective (John 15:5).

He uses lies against 1) the character of God and 2) our value/ identity in Christ (Matthew 27:43)

We believe in our hearts (Romans 10:10), but we are often desensitized to lies.

246

God knows our hearts, so we can ASK the Wonderful Counselor (Isaiah 9:6).

Lies are mostly sown in wounds. Ask the Father who we need to forgive for leading us to believe this lie. We first need to FORGIVE the offender to break the power of the lie born in the wound.

We must forgive, not just for the outward action, but for the heart wound – what we began to believe about God or ourselves as a result.

Having forgiven from the heart (Matthew 18:35), for the heart wound, then

RENOUNCE lies about God or ourselves and REPENT for agreeing and partnering with enemy and giving the lie authority.

RECEIVING FROM GOD

Ask and RECEIVE from God, truth that will ignite your heart– to replace the lies believed there:
- Intentionally move over in your heart to embrace what God is saying.
- Unpack with Him what He says. Ask Him questions until it is practical and helpful.
- Declare and REJOICE in the truth He speaks until it resonates in your heart and your heart is full.

Then our minds will be renewed and our hearts strengthened to both recognize and resist lies and temptations, hindrances to enjoyable intimacy with God. We are then able to thrive in Him.

IN A MOMENT

When we notice we are moved from peace and rest, reject any negative thought.

Simply turn to Jesus and ask: *What do You have for my heart right now?* Receive it and rejoice (aloud if possible)!

FOR ACCESS TO THE FOLLOWING RESOURCES

GO TO tendingyourheart.com

Tending Your Heart Card

Here is a link to print the Tending Your Heart Card that provides simple prompts and outlines that have proven valuable for personal use and discipleship.

Tending Your Heart for Small Groups

This is a brief 4-part video series with journaling exercises and leaders guides that provides a basic, practical and helpful introduction to hearing from and processing with God. Approximately 1 hour for each part.
It includes: Invitation to Intimacy
Challenges in Hearing
Overcoming Wounds and Lies
Tending Your Heart

Tending Your Heart for Discipleship Schools

This material has been used of the Lord to launch many Jesus followers into more life-giving intimacy with Him. It includes videos, resources and journaling exercises incorporating most of the essentials in this book. Total 6+ hours.

HELP OTHERS FIND THIS BOOK!

If you have found this book helpful, we would be very grateful if you would go to Amazon.com and write a review.

This will increase the exposure of *Wholehearted!* and make it easier for readers to find it.

And please spread the word through your social network!

Thank you!